Simon Newcomb, George William Hill

Papers relating to the transit of Venus in 1874: Prepared

under the direction of the Commission

Part 1-3

Simon Newcomb, George William Hill

Papers relating to the transit of Venus in 1874: Prepared under the direction of the Commission
Part 1-3

ISBN/EAN: 9783337197315

Printed in Europe, USA, Canada, Australia, Japan

Cover: Foto ©ninafisch / pixelio.de

More available books at **www.hansebooks.com**

INVESTIGATION

OF

CORRECTIONS TO HANSEN'S TABLES OF THE MOON;

WITH

TABLES FOR THEIR APPLICATION.

BY

SIMON NEWCOMB,

PROFESSOR, U. S. NAVY.

FORMING PART III OF PAPERS PUBLISHED BY THE COMMISSION ON THE TRANSIT OF VENUS.

———————

WASHINGTON:
GOVERNMENT PRINTING OFFICE.
1876.

TABLE OF CONTENTS.

696

INTRODUCTORY NOTE.

When the problem of utilizing the observations of occultations at the several Transit of Venus stations, so as to determine the longitudes of those stations with all attainable accuracy, was presented to the Commission on the Transit of Venus, it was found necessary to make a careful determination of the errors of the lunar ephemeris before an entirely satisfactory solution of the problem could be attempted. The Secretary of the Commission was therefore charged with this work, most of the computations on which have been made under his direction by Mr. D. P. Todd, computer for the Commission.

WASHINGTON, *May* 25, 1876.

CORRECTIONS TO BE APPLIED TO HANSEN'S TABLES OF THE MOON.

§ 1.

INVESTIGATION OF ERRORS OF LONGITUDE.

One of the most important operations in connection with the observations of the transit of Venus is the accurate determination of the longitudes of the stations. Many of these stations are so far removed from telegraphic communication that the longitudes must depend mainly on the moon. Determinations of longitude from moon culminations are found by experience to be subject to constant errors which it is difficult to determine and allow for. It was therefore a part of the policy of the American Commission to depend on occultations rather than upon moon culminations for the determination of longitudes. The reason for this course is, that the disappearance of a star behind the limb of the moon is a sudden phenomenon, the time of which can always be fixed within a fraction of a second. If the ephemeris of the moon and star were correct, and the disk of the former a perfect circle, the longitude could be determined from the occultation with the same degree of accuracy that the phenomenon could be observed. The question arises, how far these sources of error can be diminished. The inequalities of the lunar surface form a source of error which it is impossible to avoid, but which is comparatively innocuous when many observations are made, since the errors will be purely accidental, and will therefore be eliminated from the mean of a great number of observations.

The position of the star can be determined by meridian observations with almost any required degree of accuracy. We have, then, only to see how far the errors of the lunar ephemeris can be diminished; and to reduce these errors to a minimum is the object of the present paper.

Hansen's tables are taken for this purpose, because there is reason to believe that the perturbations on which these tables are founded are, in the main, extremely accurate; more accurate and complete, in fact, than any others which have been tabulated. Still, before they can be used for the purpose in question, a number of very important corrections are required, which we may divide into two classes,—corrections to the theory, and to the elements.

It is well known that Hansen increased all the perturbations of his tables by the constant factor 0.0001544, on account of a supposed want of coincidence between the center of figure and the center of gravity of the moon. I have shown that Hansen fails to sustain this position, and that there is no good reason to suppose that the moon differs from any other of the heavenly bodies in this respect.* Our first course would therefore be to diminish all of Hansen's inequalities by this factor, were it not that there are reasons why each of the two greatest perturbations of the moon's motion,—the evection and the variation,—should be found larger from observation than he found them from theory.

Evection.—The evection has the eccentricity as a factor; the value of the other factor being nearly o.4. If, then, the adopted eccentricity of the moon be erroneous, the computed evection will be erroneous by four-tenths the amount of the error. Now, by reference to Hansen's *"Darlegung der theoretischen Berechnung der in den Mondtafeln angewandten Störungen"*† (page 173), it will be seen that the eccentricity adopted throughout in the computation of the perturbations of the moon is less by 0.0000073 than the value he finally found from observation, and adopted in the tables. Had he used the latter value, the theoretical evection would have been greater by the fraction $\frac{.0000073}{.0549008} = 0.000133$. The factor actually used being 0.0001544, the evection, thus increased, is too large by only 0.000021 of its entire amount, or $0''.09$. Consequently, the tabular coefficient of evection should be diminished by this amount. Precisely the same result follows, if we adopt Hansen's view of a separation of the centers of figure and gravity of the moon; and Hansen himself is led to it on page 175 of the work cited, only instead of $0''.09$, he says, "kein volles Zehntheil einer Secunde."

Variation.—That the coefficient of variation resulting from meridian observations will be greater than the actual coefficient may be anticipated from the following considerations. The inequality in question attains its maxima and minima in the moon's octants. In the first octant, we have a maximum. The elongation of the moon from the sun is then about 3^h; and the observed position of the moon is mainly dependent on observations of the first limb made in the daytime, when the apparent semi-diameter of the moon will be diminished by the brilliancy of the surrounding sky. No account of this diminution of the apparent semi-diameter being taken in the reductions, the semi-diameter actually applied is too large, and the observed right ascension of the moon is also too large.

When the moon reaches the third octant, the value of the variation attains its minimum. The moon then transits at 9^h, and the meridian observation is made on the first limb, while the apparent semi-diameter is increased by the irradiation consequent upon the contrast between the moon and the sky. The result will be that the observed right ascension will be too small.

The same causes will make the observed right ascension too great in the fifth octant, and too small in the seventh. These positive and negative errors of observed right ascension correspond to the times of maximum and minimum effects of variation in increasing the longitude of the moon. Therefore, the observed variation will appa-

* Proceedings of the American Association for the Advancement of Science, 1868.—Silliman's American Journal of Science, November, 1868.

† Abhandlungen der mathematisch-physischen Classe der Königlich-Sächsischen Gesellschaft der Wissenschaften Band vi.

rently be larger than the actual variation, whatever this may be. This seems a much more natural and probable cause for the apparent excess of the observed over the theoretical perturbations than that assigned by Hansen. Hansen's factor only increases the coefficient in question by o″.33; but it seems probable that the variation derived from observations alone would be yet larger than Hansen's increased variation. In fact, in 1867, I found, by comparing the errors of the lunar ephemeris when the moon culminated at different times of the day, that the effect of the greater irradiation at night was very strongly marked. During the four years 1862–65 the 'mean errors of the tables in right ascension at different times of day were as follows:*

$$
\begin{array}{lr}
\text{Before sunset} \dots\dots\dots\dots\dots\dots & -\text{o. }154 \\
\text{After bright daylight in the evening} \dots\dots & -\text{o.093} \\
\text{Before bright daylight in the morning} \dots. & +\text{o.091} \\
\text{After sunrise} \dots\dots\dots\dots\dots\dots & +\text{o. }153 \\
\end{array}
$$

In the difference between the results for each limb, the effect of increased irradiation seems to be o″.06.

The only remaining term which is large enough to be materially affected by the increase in question is the annual equation, of which the increase is o″.10.

A glance at the errors of Hansen's tables, given by meridian observations, will show that the errors about the time of first quarter, and, indeed, during the first half of the lunation, are in the mean less by between 3″ and 4″ than during the second half. Hence, either the semi-diameter, or the parallactic equation, or both, are too large. The parallactic equation used by Hansen corresponds to a value 8″.916 for the solar parallax, which value is too large by probably not much less than o″.10. The result which I deduced in 1867 from all the really valuable data extant was 8″.848; and the determinations which have since been made, when revised with the best data, seem to indicate a diminution of this value rather than an increase. These indications are, however, as yet, a little too indefinite to predicate anything upon. I shall therefore continue to use 8″.848, which will diminish Hansen's value by o″.068. The corresponding diminution in the principal parallactic term will be o″.96, while there will be two other terms to receive a smaller diminution.

This correction will still leave a difference of about 2″ between the results from the first and second limbs, which will be accounted for by an error of 1″ in the adopted semi-diameter. This correction to the semi-diameter is *a priori* quite probable, as the improved meridian instruments of the present time give a semi-diameter of the sun 1″ less than the older ones from which the diameters adopted in our ephemerides were derived. It is to be expected that the semi-diameter of the moon will exhibit a similar apparent diminution.

From a note in Hansen's *Darlegung* (page 439), it will be seen that one of the terms in the true longitude has crept into the tables with a wrong sign. As employed in the tables, and given on page 15 of the introduction, it is, $+\text{o}''.335 \sin (2g - 4g' + 2\omega - 4\omega')$.
As revised in the *Darlegung*, it is $\dots\dots\dots -\text{o}''.285 \sin \dots\dots\dots\dots\dots$
Therefore the tables need the correction $\dots. -\text{o}''.62 \sin \dots\dots\dots\dots\dots$

---

* Investigation of the Distance of the Sun, p. 24.

The following is a list of the corrections we have so far deduced to Hansen's tables. They should in strictness be applied to the mean longitude, or "*Argument fondamental*", but they may without serious error be applied to the true longitude.

Put

    D, the argument of parallactic inequality, or mean elongation of the moon from the sun;

    g, the moon's mean anomaly;

    g', the sun's mean anomaly;

    ω, the distance of the moon's perigee from the ascending node;

    ω', the distance of the sun's perigee from the same node.

We then have

$$D = g - g' + \omega - \omega',$$

and the corrections in question are,

$$
\begin{aligned}
&+0.96 \sin D \\
&+0.07 \sin (D - g) \\
&-0.13 \sin (D + g')
\end{aligned}
\quad \text{\} Parallactic terms.}
$$

$$+0.09 \sin g' \qquad \text{Annual equation.}$$

$$-0.33 \sin 2D \qquad \text{Variation.}$$

$$-0.10 \sin (2D - g) \qquad \text{Evection.}$$

$$-0.62 \sin (g2 - 4g' + 2\omega - 4\omega') \qquad \text{Accidental error.}$$

The fourth and fifth terms of this expression have the effect to remove the increase which Hansen applied to his inequalities on account of the position of the center of gravity of the moon, while the sixth is the result of the slight error of the eccentricity which he employed in computing the coefficient of evection.

In comparing with meridian observations which have been reduced without any correction to the apparent semi-diameter depending on the time of day, the correction of variation may also be omitted, since a yet larger apparent correction, having the opposite algebraic sign, will result from the apparent variations of that semi-diameter, as already explained.

As regards the possible corrections to the elements of Hansen's tables, it is to be remarked that that investigator did not avail himself of the elements of the lunar orbit deduced by Airy from the Greenwich observations between 1750 and 1830, but obtained his final values of the elements by a comparison of his own. Of the nature and extent of the observations thus employed, we have no details; but it is not likely that more than a very small fraction of the entire mass of observations was used, and it can therefore hardly be expected that the elements were determined with the last degree of accuracy. Any error in the motion of the perigee or node will constantly increase with the time. If, in addition to this, we reflect that the meridian observations of the last twenty years are far more accurate than those Hansen had at his disposal, it will not seem at all surprising to find quite sensible errors in the present longitudes of the lunar perigee and node as derived by Hansen. Our next step will therefore be to determine what corrections to Hansen's elements are indicated by the recent observations of the moon made at Greenwich and Washington since 1862, a period during which both series of observations are carefully compared with Hansen's tables.

The general ideas on which the present investigation of these corrections is based are these: the errors of the moon's tabular longitude are of two classes,—a progressive correction, which apparently increases uniformly with the time; and errors of short period, the principal ones of which go through their period during one revolution of the moon or less. In determining the errors of the first class from observation, those of the second class may be regarded as accidental errors, the effect of which will be eliminated from the mean of a large number of observations. Since, in a series of observations extending through a number of years, the maxima and minima of each term of short period will fall indiscriminately into all parts of all the other periods, each periodic correction may be determined as if the effects of the others were purely accidental errors. At the same time, as the elimination of each periodic error from the maxima and minima of all the others cannot be complete in any finite time, it is desirable that each periodic correction of sensible magnitude which we can determine beforehand shall be applied to the residuals before the latter are used to determine the corrections to the elements.

The corrections of the elements of longitude have been made to depend principally upon the observed right ascensions, instead of reducing the observed errors of right ascension and polar distance to errors of longitude and latitude. The reason for this course is, that the apparent errors of polar distance, after correcting them approximately for errors of the elements easily determined, will arise principally from errors of observation, and not from errors of the tables. In fact, the observations of the moon's declination are sometimes affected with accidental errors of a magnitude which it is difficult to account for, especially in the case of Washington. Granting that the moon moves in a plane the position of which can be very accurately determined, we have afterward only to determine the moon's position in that plane, and this can be done from an observed right ascension almost as well as if we had a directly observed longitude. The longitude thus determined will be less likely to be affected with systematic errors than if we suppose the position entirely unknown, and change the errors of right ascension and declination to errors of longitude and latitude, without regard to the possible constant errors of the measured declinations.

Formulæ for expressing the longitude and latitude of the moon in terms of the lunar elements are given by Hansen in a posthumous memoir.* The following terms are sufficient for our present purpose :

Put

l, the moon's longitude in orbit ;

θ, the longitude of the ascending node ;

i, the inclination of the orbit to the ecliptic ;

a, δ, the moon's right ascension and declination ;

ω, the obliquity of the ecliptic.

---

* Ueber die Darstellung der graden Aufsteigung und Abweichung des Mondes in Function der Länge in der Bahn und der Knotenlänge. Abhandlungen der Königlich-Sächsischen Gesellschaft der Wissenschaften, Bd. z, No. viii.

We then have, approximately,

$$\alpha = l - 2°.5 \sin 2l - 1°.1 \sin (2l - \theta) + 1°.1 \sin \theta$$
$$\sin \delta = \sin \omega \sin l + \cos \omega \sin i \sin (l - \theta)$$
$$= 0.40 \sin l + 0.08 \sin (l - \theta)$$

The differential co-efficients derived from these expressions are,

$$\frac{d\alpha}{dl} = 1 - 0.037 \cos (2l - \theta) - 0.087 \cos 2l$$

$$\frac{d\alpha}{d\theta} = 0.018 \cos \theta + 0018 \cos (2l - \theta)$$

$$\frac{d\alpha}{di} = 0.21 \sin \theta - 0.21 \sin (2l - \theta)$$

$$\cos \delta \frac{d\delta}{dl} = 0.40 \cos l + 0.08 \cos (l - \theta)$$
$$= (0.40 + 0.08 \cos \theta) \cos l + 0.08 \sin \theta \sin l$$

$$\cos \delta \frac{d\delta}{d\theta} = - 0.081 \cos (l - \theta)$$

$$\cos \delta \frac{d\delta}{di} = 0.92 \sin (l - \theta)$$

From the first three formulæ, it will be seen, that the mean error in right ascension is very nearly the same as the mean error in longitude; the periodic corrections being supposed to be eliminated from this mean.

The investigation of the corrections from observations is now made as follows: All the apparent errors of the tables derived from the meridian observations at Greenwich and Washington since 1862 have been collected, arranged in the order of dates and the mean taken for each year; observations of the separate limbs being kept separate. The mean error in right ascension for each year is as follows:

Apparent errors of Hansen's tables in R. A.

Year.	Greenwich.			Washington.			Mean.		
	I.	II.	Diff.	I.	II.	Diff.	I.	II.	Mean.
	"	"	"	"	"	"	"	"	"
1862	..	..	..	..	..	..	− 3.6	− 0.6	− 2.1
1863	..	..	..	..	..	..	− 2.3	+ 0.5	− 0.9
1864	..	..	..	..	..	..	− 1.0	+ 1.8	+ 0.4
1865	− 0.2	+ 3.0	3.2	+ 0.3	+ 3.9	3.6	0.0	+ 3.4	+ 1.7
1866	+ 1.2	+ 3.6	2.4	+ 0.9	+ 4.5	3.6	+ 1.0	+ 4.0	+ 2.5
1867	+ 2.4	+ 5.7	3.3	+ 2.4	+ 5.8	3.4	+ 2.4	+ 5.8	+ 4.1
1868	+ 2.6	+ 6.0	3.4	+ 2.4	+ 6.6	4.2	+ 2.5	+ 6.3	+ 4.4
1869	+ 3.3	+ 5.6	2.3	+ 7	+ 7.4	4.0	+ 3.4	+ 6.5	+ 4.9
1870	+ 3.4	+ 6.6	3.2	+ 4.6	+ 7.2	2.6	+ 4.0	+ 6.9	+ 5.4
1871	+ 5.4	+ 8.2	2.8	+ 5.1	+ 7.8	2.7	+ 5.2	+ 8.0	+ 6.6
1872	+ 6.0	+ 8.7	2.7	+ 6.2	+ 9.6	3.4	+ 6.1	+ 9.2	+ 7.6
1873	+ 6.9	+ 9.4	2.5	+ 6.9	+10.2	3.3	+ 6.9	+10.2	+ 8.6
1874	+ 8.1	+11.4	3.3	+ 7.1	+10.8	3.7	+ 7.6	+11.1	+ 9.4

The last column exhibits the apparent tabular errors in mean right ascension, and therefore in mean longitude, as derived each year from all the observations. The sudden apparent alteration of nearly one second per annum in the mean motion of the moon, exhibited in this column, seems to me one of the most extraordinary of astronomical phenomena; but, as I have discussed it in several papers during the last five years, I shall do no more here than call attention to its continuance, and to the impossibility of representing it by any small number of periodic terms without introducing discordances into the longitude during previous years.

It will be seen that there are discordances between the results of the two observatories, sometimes amounting to more than a second. In determining the corrections of short period, it is desirable to reduce the systematic errors extending through each year to a minimum; the question whether such errors are in the theory or the observations being indifferent. It is also desirable that in taking the mean of the results of the two observatories, they should be made comparable with each other by correcting either of them for the systematic difference. These corrections, of course, only admit of approximate determination, and they have been applied each year to that observatory or that limb of the moon in which, judging from the deviations from uniform progression, it was judged most likely that the discordance existed. The following are the corrections actually applied to the several classes of tabular errors:

Year.	Greenwich.		Washington.	
	I.	II.	I.	II.
	s.	s.	s.	s.
1862–63	+ 0.06	+ 0.06	0	0.00
1864	0	0	0	0
1865–68	0	0	0	− 0.04
1869	0	+ 0.06	0	− 0.04
1870	+ 0.06	0	0	− 0.04
1871	0	0	0	0
1872	0	0	0	− 0.04
1873–74	0	0	0	0

Having applied these corrections throughout their several years, the Greenwich and Washington observations were considered strictly comparable; and when the moon was observed at both observatories on the same day, the mean of the corrected tabular errors was taken. The mean outstanding tabular error for each year now becomes as follows:

Year.	$\delta\lambda$	Year.	$\delta\lambda$	Year.	$\delta\lambda$	Year.	$\delta\lambda$
1862	− 2.1	1866	+ 2.2	1869	+ 5.1	1872	+ 7.3
1863	− 0.9	1867	+ 3.8	1870	+ 5.6	1873	+ 8.6
1864	+ 0.4	1868	+ 4.1	1871	+ 6.6	1874	+ 9.7
1865	+ 1.4						

These quantities, with the sign changed, should be considered as corrections to the fundamental argument, and we have to determine the corresponding correction to the right ascensions which are to be applied to the individual tabular errors. To reduce them to corrections of true longitude, they are to be multiplied by the factor

$$1 + 2e \cos g = 1 + 0.11 \cos g$$

The corresponding factor for correction of right ascension is, with sufficient approximation,

$$\delta\alpha = (1 + 0.11 \cos g - 0.04 \cos (2l - \theta) - 0.09 \cos 2l)\, \delta\lambda$$

In this formula, $\delta\lambda$ represents the correction to the mean longitude, while we may suppose l to represent indifferently the mean or the true longitude; and, during a period of several months at a time, we may represent the longitude as a function of g. The value of $\delta\alpha$ has been reduced to a table of double entry as a function of g and of the time. To express the mean longitude as a function of g, we have

$$l = g + \pi$$
$$2l - \theta = 2g + 2\pi - \theta$$
$$2l = 2g + 2\pi$$

By the substitution of these values, the expression for $\delta\alpha$ becomes

$$\delta\alpha = (1 + 0.11 \cos g + A \cos 2g + B \sin 2g)\, \delta\lambda$$

where

$$A = -.04 \cos (2\pi - \theta) - .09 \cos 2\pi$$
$$B = .04 \sin (2\pi - \theta) + .09 \sin 2\pi$$

The values of π, θ, A, and B for periods of six months are as follow:

Year.	π	θ	A	B	Year.	π	θ	A	B
	°	°				°	°		
1862.0	226	274	+ .05	+ .09	1869.0	153	139	— .01	— .06
1862.5	248	264	+ .09	+ .09	1869.5	173	129	— .07	— .05
1863.0	269	255	+ .08	— .04	1870.0	194	119	— .08	.00
1863.5	289	245	+ .03	— .08	1870.5	214	110	— .06	+ .05
1864.0	309	235	— .02	— .07	1871.0	234	100	— .01	+ .09
1864.5	330	226	— .05	— .04	1871.5	255	90	+ .06	+ .08
1865.0	350	216	— .06	.00	1872.0	275	81	+ .10	+ .02
1865.5	310	206	— .05	+ .03	1872.5	295	71	+ .09	— .06
1866.0	31	197	— .01	+ .08	1873.0	316	61	+ .08	— .11
1866.5	51	187	+ .02	+ .05	1873.5	336	52	— .05	— .11
1867.0	71	177	+ .05	+ .03	1874.0	356	42	— .12	— .04
1867.5	92	168	+ .05	.00	1874.5	17	32	— .12	+ .05
1868.0	112	158	+ .04	— .02	1875.0	37	23	— .04	+ .12
1868.5	133	148	+ .03	— .05					

The coefficient $1 + 0.11 \cos g + A \cos 2g + B \sin 2g$ is next tabulated for each of these sets of values of A and B for every 10° of g, and multiplied by the corresponding value of $\delta\lambda$. As these tables are superseded by those given at the close of this paper, it is not necessary to print them.

The corrections of short period, which have been actually applied, are

$$+ 0.96 \sin D$$
$$- 0.13 \sin (D + g')$$
$$+ 0.09 \sin g'$$
$$- 0.62 \sin (2g - 4g' + 2\omega - 4\omega')$$

The first three have been combined into a single one of double argument, in which the arguments are D and the month; the latter corresponding to g'. The terms dependent on this argument are so small that they may be regarded as constant during an entire month.

In this same table is included a partially conjectural correction for the variations of the moon's semi-diameter. The correction to Hansen's value has been assumed as $-2''.0$, when the moon is in the neighborhood of the sun, so that her limb is very faint; and as $-0''.4$ after the close of evening twilight. Between two hours of elongation and the close of twilight, it is assumed to increase uniformly. The sum of these four corrections is given in the following table:

Days before mean full moon.	FIRST LIMB.												Days before mean full moon.
	Jan.	Feb.	Mar.	April.	May.	June.	July.	Aug.	Sept.	Oct.	Nov.	Dec.	
	''	''	''	''	''	''	''	''	''	''	''	''	
− 14	+ 2.4	+ 2.5	+ 2.5	+ 2.6	+ 2.5	+ 2.4	+ 2.3	+ 2.2	+ 2.1	+ 2.1	+ 2.2	+ 2.3	− 14
− 13	+ 2.3	+ 2.4	+ 2.5	+ 2.5	+ 2.4	+ 2.3	+ 2.2	+ 2.1	+ 2.0	+ 2.0	+ 2.1	+ 2.2	− 13
− 12	+ 2.2	+ 2.3	+ 2.5	+ 2.4	+ 2.4	+ 2.3	+ 2.2	+ 2.1	+ 2.0	+ 1.9	+ 2.0	+ 2.0	− 12
− 11	+ 2.1	+ 2.2	+ 2.4	+ 2.4	+ 2.3	+ 2.2	+ 2.1	+ 2.1	+ 2.0	+ 1.8	+ 1.9	+ 2.0	− 11
− 10	+ 2.0	+ 2.1	+ 2.4	+ 2.3	+ 2.2	+ 2.1	+ 2.0	+ 2.0	+ 2.0	+ 1.7	+ 1.7	+ 1.8	− 10
− 9	+ 1.8	+ 2.0	+ 2.3	+ 2.2	+ 2.1	+ 2.1	+ 2.0	+ 1.9	+ 1.8	+ 1.6	+ 1.5	+ 1.6	− 9
− 8	+ 1.5	+ 1.7	+ 2.1	+ 2.0	+ 2.0	+ 2.0	+ 1.9	+ 1.8	+ 1.7	+ 1.4	+ 1.4	+ 1.5	− 8
− 7	+ 1.5	+ 1.5	+ 1.8	+ 1.8	+ 1.8	+ 1.8	+ 1.7	+ 1.6	+ 1.4	+ 1.3	+ 1.4	+ 1.5	− 7
− 6	+ 1.5	+ 1.4	+ 1.4	+ 1.5	+ 1.6	+ 1.5	+ 1.5	+ 1.4	+ 1.2	+ 1.3	+ 1.4	+ 1.4	− 6
− 5	+ 1.4	+ 1.3	+ 1.3	+ 1.8	+ 1.4	+ 1.4	+ 1.3	+ 1.1	+ 1.2	+ 1.2	+ 1.3	+ 1.4	− 5
− 4	+ 1.2	+ 1.2	+ 1.2	+ 1.1	+ 1.1	+ 1.1	+ 1.0	+ 1.1	+ 1.1	+ 1.1	+ 1.2	+ 1.2	− 4
− 3	+ 1.1	+ 1.0	+ 1.0	+ 1.0	+ 0.9	+ 0.9	+ 0.9	+ 1.0	+ 1.0	+ 1.0	+ 1.1	+ 1.1	− 3
− 2	+ 0.9	+ 0.8	+ 0.8	+ 0.8	+ 0.7	+ 0.7	+ 0.8	+ 0.8	+ 0.8	+ 0.8	+ 0.9	+ 0.9	− 2
− 1	+ 0.6	+ 0.6	+ 0.6	+ 0.6	+ 0.6	+ 0.6	+ 0.6	+ 0.6	+ 0.6	+ 0.6	+ 0.7	+ 0.6	− 1
0	+ 0.4	+ 0.4	+ 0.4	+ 0.4	+ 0.4	+ 0.4	+ 0.4	+ 0.4	+ 0.4	+ 0.4	+ 0.4	+ 0.4	0

Days after mean full moon.	SECOND LIMB.												Days after mean full moon.
	Jan.	Feb.	Mar.	April.	May.	June.	July.	Aug.	Sept.	Oct.	Nov.	Dec.	
	''	''	''	''	''	''	''	''	''	''	''	''	
0	− 0.4	− 0.4	− 0.4	− 0.4	− 0.4	− 0.4	− 0.4	− 0.4	− 0.4	− 0.4	− 0.4	− 0.4	0
+ 1	− 0.6	− 0.6	− 0.6	− 0.6	− 0.6	− 0.6	− 0.6	− 0.6	− 0.6	− 0.6	− 0.6	− 0.6	+ 1
+ 2	− 0.8	− 0.7	− 0.8	− 0.8	− 0.8	− 0.8	− 0.7	− 0.7	− 0.8	− 0.8	− 0.8	− 0.8	+ 2
+ 3	− 1.1	− 0.9	− 1.0	− 1.0	− 0.9	− 0.9	− 0.9	− 0.9	− 1.0	− 1.0	− 1.0	− 1.1	+ 3
+ 4	− 1.2	− 1.1	− 1.2	− 1.1	− 1.1	− 1.0	− 1.0	− 1.1	− 1.1	− 1.2	− 1.2	− 1.2	+ 4
+ 5	− 1.4	− 1.2	− 1.2	− 1.3	− 1.4	− 1.4	− 1.4	− 1.2	− 1.3	− 1.3	− 1.4	− 1.4	+ 5
+ 6	− 1.4	− 1.3	− 1.3	− 1.4	− 1.5	− 1.5	− 1.5	− 1.5	− 1.4	− 1.4	− 1.4	− 1.5	+ 6
+ 7	− 1.5	− 1.3	− 1.6	− 1.6	− 1.7	− 1.7	− 1.8	− 1.7	− 1.6	− 1.5	− 1.5	− 1.5	+ 7
+ 8	− 1.4	− 1.5	− 1.8	− 1.8	− 1.9	− 1.9	− 2.0	− 1.9	− 1.9	− 1.7	− 1.5	− 1.5	+ 8
+ 9	− 1.7	− 1.7	− 2.0	− 1.9	− 1.9	− 2.0	− 2.1	− 2.1	− 2.1	− 1.8	− 1.8	− 1.7	+ 9
+ 10	− 1.9	− 1.9	− 2.0	− 2.0	− 2.0	− 2.1	− 2.1	− 2.2	− 2.3	− 2.1	− 2.0	− 1.9	+ 10
+ 11	− 2.0	− 1.9	− 2.1	− 2.0	− 2.0	− 2.1	− 2.2	− 2.3	− 2.4	− 2.2	− 2.2	− 2.0	+ 11
+ 12	− 2.1	− 2.0	− 2.1	− 2.0	− 2.1	− 2.2	− 2.3	− 2.4	− 2.4	− 2.4	− 2.3	− 2.1	+ 12
+ 13	− 2.2	− 2.1	− 2.1	− 2.0	− 2.1	− 2.2	− 2.3	− 2.4	− 2.5	− 2.5	− 2.4	− 2.3	+ 13
+ 14	− 2.3	− 2.2	− 2.1	− 2.1	− 2.2	− 2.3	− 2.4	− 2.5	− 2.6	− 2.5	− 2.5	− 2.4	+ 14

By the application of the foregoing corrections to the errors of the moon's tabular right ascension, these errors may be supposed to be reduced to very small quantities, depending on the errors of the lunar elements, with which they are connected by the equation

$$\delta\alpha = \frac{d\alpha}{dl}\,\delta l + \frac{d\alpha}{d\theta}\,\delta\theta + \frac{d\alpha}{di}\,\delta i,$$

the differential coefficients having the values given on page 12. When we substitute these values, the expression for $\delta\alpha$ will contain the terms

$$(+.018\,\delta\theta - .037\,\delta\alpha)\cos(2l - \theta)$$
$$-.087\,\delta\alpha\cos 2l$$
$$+.018\,\delta\theta\cos\theta$$
$$+0.21\,\delta i\sin\theta$$
$$-0.21\,\delta i\sin(2l - \theta)$$

If we represent the sum of these terms by P, we shall have
$$\delta l = \delta\alpha - P$$

In the investigation of the corrections to the moon's eccentricity and longitude of perigee, the terms of P may be entirely neglected. This arises from the circumstances that the appreciable terms of l or α arising from the errors of these elements have the same period with g, the mean anomaly, while P contains no appreciable periodic term depending on g. The outstanding portion of $\delta\alpha$ probably averages not more than one second or two at the utmost, so that the term $.037\,\delta\alpha$ is quite insignificant. The term $.018\,\delta\theta$ may have a constant value of $0''.25$, more or less;* but the short period of the term $2l - \theta$, and its incommensurability with the period of g, permit of this error being regarded as fortuitous. The same remark applies to the terms $.087\,\delta\alpha\cos 2l$ and $0.21\,\delta i\sin(2l - \theta)$. The only remaining terms have the period of θ, which is more than eighteen years. The effect of these possible errors is therefore eliminated in the mean correction for each year, which has been already applied to the errors.

To determine the correction to the eccentricity and longitude of the perigee resulting from each year's observations, the residuals in right ascension, after the application of the three corrections already described, have been arranged according to the values of the mean anomaly to which they correspond. The results are shown in the following table, which gives for certain limits of mean anomaly in the first column, firstly, the sum of the residuals (tabular *minus* observed) in right ascension, corresponding to all the values of mean anomaly between those limits; and, secondly, the number of the residuals. In taking these sums, the observations at the two observatories are counted separately, so that when observations were made at both observatories on the same date, the sum of the residuals is taken, and the observations count 2 in the column N.

* It is afterward found that the value of this product is only $0''.08$.

Sums of errors of moon's corrected right ascension, given by observations at Greenwich and Washington.

Limits of mean anomaly.	1862.		1863.		1864.		1865.	
	Σdα	N.	Σdα	N.	Σdα	N.	Σdα	N.
o to 10	+ 3.9	4	+ 21.5	10	+ 19.6	9	+ 1.4	7
10 to 20	+ 3.6	6	+ 18.3	12	+ 6.1	7	+ 3.4	4
20 to 30	− 0.2	5	+ 14.2	8	+ 5.8	5	− 0.3	10
30 to 40	+ 9.3	6	+ 25.7	11	+ 4.5	7	− 0.5	5
40 to 50	+ 2.7	8	+ 9.0	8	+ 2.6	3	− 3.6	6
50 to 60	+ 0.3	8	+ 9.8	9	− 1.6	10	− 1.1	6
60 to 70	+ 8.9	10	− 4.3	7	+ 0.7	5	− 6.1	7
70 to 80	− 3.7	4	+ 7.0	10	− 7.0	6	− 6.7	6
80 to 90	+ 6.7	7	− 6.7	6	− 11.8	9	− 6.1	6
90 to 100	+ 3.9	6	− 5.3	9	− 3.4	6	− 8.5	7
100 to 110	+ 3.9	11	− 0.4	5	− 8.1	5	− 0.7	5
110 to 120	− 6.4	9	− 3.9	8	− 3.0	3	− 7.5	6
120 to 130	− 3.2	8	− 3.9	7	+ 0.1	5	− 5.5	6
130 to 140	− 7.8	6	− 6.8	8	− 12.2	7	+ 5.0	5
140 to 150	− 0.9	5	− 15.9	8	+ 0.9	3	+ 1.1	5
150 to 160	− 0.1	5	− 18.2	9	− 6.7	7	+ 1.5	4
160 to 170	− 8.8	4	− 19.7	6	+ 2.5	6	+ 4.3	5
170 to 180	− 5.7	4	− 9.9	7	− 5.3	5	+ 6.4	6
180 to 190	− 17.4	9	− 33.1	14	− 8.6	7	+ 8.9	6
190 to 200	− 15.5	7	− 4.3	4	− 0.6	4	+ 13.2	8
200 to 210	− 3.8	10	− 1.0	6	− 6.4	9	+ 7.8	8
210 to 220	− 0.2	8	− 1.9	9	− 8.9	8	+ 13.1	7
220 to 230	− 28.9	9	− 7.5	10	+ 3.6	7	+ 5.1	5
230 to 240	− 7.5	7	− 1.9	7	+ 0.8	7	+ 10.3	5
240 to 250	+ 13.0	8	+ 0.4	9	+ 1.6	7	+ 7.5	8
250 to 260	− 2.0	4	+ 7.6	8	+ 11.5	8	+ 7.3	7
260 to 270	+ 1.6	9	+ 1.4	5	+ 11.7	7	+ 16.2	12
270 to 280	+ 3.7	5	+ 11.3	9	+ 25.3	11	+ 7.6	11
280 to 290	+ 4.7	7	+ 0.8	5	+ 18.2	8	+ 9.6	8
290 to 300	− 1.3	1	+ 15.9	7	+ 6.6	4	+ 5.8	11
300 to 310	+ 3.0	3	+ 23.5	9	+ 7.8	6	+ 10.1	7
310 to 320	+ 8.3	2	+ 22.6	6	+ 6.4	5	+ 16.4	10
320 to 330	− 1.8	5	+ 18.2	9	+ 11.6	7	+ 14.5	7
330 to 340	+ 9.5	6	+ 1.2	7	+ 18.5	10	+ 16.7	11
340 to 350	+ 11.8	8	+ 7.2	7	+ 4.2	7	+ 7.6	7
350 to 360	+ 13.6	5	+ 14.4	8	+ 16.5	6	+ 5.3	9
	+106.4	225	+222.0	267	+187.1	236	+205.9	255
	−116.0		−144.7		− 71.0		− 46.6	
	− 9.6		+ 78.3		+116.1		+159.3	

Sums of errors of moon's corrected right ascension, &c.—Continued.

Limits of mean anomaly.	1866.		1867.		1868.		1869.	
	Σδa	N.	Σδa	N.	Σδa	N.	Σδa	N.
° °	"		"		"		"	
0 to 10	− 1.7	6	+ 7.4	5	− 4.2	4	− 10.7	4
10 to 20	− 2.5	4	− 5.0	2	+ 3.9	7	− 4.2	4
20 to 30	− 7.5	3	− 1.7	4	− 2.5	3	− 0.8	6
30 to 40	− 7.1	5	− 7.5	3	− 9.4	6	+ 4.2	5
40 to 50	− 14.5	7	+ 5.5	4	− 9.0	5	+ 11.0	6
50 to 60	− 0.7	1	− 2.0	4	− 0.7	7	+ 5.5	3
60 to 70	+ 1.3	5	− 8.5	4	+ 2.2	7	+ 3.1	5
70 to 80	+ 5.3	6	− 4.8	3	+ 4.1	8	+ 7.7	7
80 to 90	+ 1.6	6	− 3.6	1	+ 12.2	7	+ 8.0	8
90 to 100	+ 3.9	4	+ 2.6	5	− 0.3	4	+ 16.8	8
100 to 110	+ 4.4	9	− 0.6	5	+ 14.9	7	+ 5.1	9
110 to 120	+ 4.8	8	+ 3.9	5	+ 9.8	6	+ 8.3	6
120 to 130	− 5.4	8	+ 1.6	7	+ 4.1	5	+ 14.5	7
130 to 140	+ 3.4	6	+ 4.1	6	+ 10.2	8	+ 7.5	8
140 to 150	+ 10.1	9	+ 1.9	7	+ 5.2'	7	+ 3.1	6
150 to 160	− 4.1	6	− 2.6	7	+ 2.1	9	+ 20.3	7
160 to 170	+ 3.3	7	+ 6.8	5	+ 1.3	8	+ 3.7	3
170 to 180	− 0.1	7	− 5.0	8	+ 0.8	7	+ 12.2	7
180 to 190	+ 0.8	6	− 0.3	2	+ 12.3	8	+ 7.0	5
190 to 200	+ 5.9	6	+ 2.0	4	+ 17.9	6	+ 6.3	4
200 to 210	− 3.2	6	+ 2.8	6	+ 5.2	5	+ 10.1	5
210 to 220	+ 0.3	6	− 1.7	4	+ 13.0	8	+ 12.2	5
220 to 230	− 5.4	4	+ 12.9	9	+ 4.8	4	+ 12.3	7
230 to 240	+ 4.1	8	+ 8.2	6	+ 15.2	9	− 1.3	3
240 to 250	− 1.8	7	+ 25.4	9	+ 7.4	8	− 6.4	6
250 to 260	+ 9.4	7	+ 0.9	3	+ 14.2	8	− 3.6	2
260 to 270	+ 2.7	7	+ 11.7	6	− 5.0	2	− 17.3	7
270 to 280	+ 9.7	4	+ 3.3	4	+ 1.0	7	− 18.8	5
280 to 290	+ 11.6	12	+ 7.0	7	− 9.1	5	− 21.4	6
290 to 300	+ 4.0	4	+ 0.7	3	− 3.2	8	− 13.6	3
300 to 310	+ 6 7	4	+ 16.5	7	− 8.0	2	− 4.8	2
310 to 320	+ 3.4	2	+ 2.3	5	− 11.8	8	− 0.8	1
320 to 330	+ 7.7	5	+ 0.2	5	− 10.6	9	− 4.2	2
330 to 340	+ 9.1	5	+ 3.5	6	− 11.7	6	− 18.5	6
340 to 350	+ 10.8	6	− 5.4	7	− 9.8	5	− 10.6	4
350 to 360	+ 9.2	7	− 7.2	4	− 18.3	6	− 2.2	5
	+132.9	213	+131.2	182	+161.8	229	+178.9	187
	− 54.0		− 55.9		−115.6		−139.2	
	+ 78.9		+ 75.3		+ 46.2		+ 39.7	

Sums of errors of moon's corrected right ascension, &c.—Concluded.

Limits of mean anomaly.	1870 Σδα	N.	1871. Σδα	N.	1872. Σδα	N.	1873. Σδα	N.	1874. Σδα	N.
0 to 10	− 7.8	5	− 3.8	5	+ 6.5	6	− 4.3	6	+ 4.6	4
10 to 20	− 8.8	5	+ 1.7	11	+ 8.5	10	+ 5.8	4	+ 5.9	5
20 to 30	+ 5.1	6	− 0.3	7	+ 5.5	8	+ 5.8	8	+ 18.5	6
30 to 40	+ 10.7	8	+ 6.4	7	+ 11.8	7	+ 3.4	3	+ 5.1	5
40 to 50	+ 11.8	8	+ 16.7	9	+ 6.0	4	+ 6.6	4	+ 4.4	5
50 to 60	− 7.1	5	+ 9.7	6	+ 13.8	6	+ 4.1	7	+ 8.1	5
60 to 70	+ 1.0	9	+ 18.9	8	+ 10.4	3	+ 13.4	6	+ 10.1	4
70 to 80	− 8.6	5	+ 10.8	7	+ 18.4	8	+ 13.5	3	+ 6.6	6
80 to 90	+ 18.0	12	+ 11.7	5	+ 11.3	4	+ 15.8	7	+ 6.0	3
90 to 100	+ 10.1	8	+ 18.5	3	+ 9.8	4	+ 5.1	3	+ 5.9	7
100 to 110	+ 10.8	4	+ 19.7	8	+ 13.0	6	+ 1.5	3	+ 10.9	6
110 to 120	+ 5.8	6	+ 8.8	4	+ 18.7	6	+ 5.3	8	+ 4.6	4
120 to 130	+ 10.1	7	+ 9.7	5	+ 18.3	7	+ 6.1	5	− 4.7	6
130 to 140	+ 10.1	5	+ 15.4	5	+ 0.8	8	+ 3.3	3	+ 1.8	3
140 to 150	+ 18.8	8	+ 8.1	3	+ 8.9	3	+ 8.4	5	− 0.8	7
150 to 160	+ 4.4	3	+ 3.0	7	+ 8.1	8	− 3.9	3	+ 1.3	5
160 to 170	+ 8.8	5	+ 8.7	4	+ 6.6	5	− 5.4	4	− 10.1	9
170 to 180	+ 6.9	3	+ 6.8	6	− 1.2	3	− 1.7	3	− 1.0	6
180 to 190	+ 1.8	1	+ 3.9	4	+ 1.9	4	− 2.2	4	+ 5.0	6
190 to 200	+ 7.5	4	+ 3.5	3	− 1.8	5	− 6.6	6	− 1.0	2
200 to 210	+ 8.1	5	+ 1.0	3	− 8.8	6	− 0.9	8	+ 3.7	6
210 to 220	− 8.3	8	− 8.6	8	+ 1.8	3	− 6.6	3	− 5.0	5
220 to 230	− 8.5	3	− 9.3	7	− 7.8	5	− 0.1	4	− 16.0	7
230 to 240	− 0.4	5	− 3.8	6	− 4.8	5	− 3.5	1	− 13.5	4
240 to 250	− 9.7	5	− 9.1	8	− 6.5	3	− 7.5	5	− 15.1	8
250 to 260	− 18.1	6	− 5.8	5	− 9.1	4	− 7.1	4	− 83.0	5
260 to 270	− 8.3	8	− 4.6	5	− 13.8	8	− 8.6	3	− 88.6	4
270 to 280	− 18.9	8	− 7.1	7	− 8.4	5	− 4.3	4	− 15.6	4
280 to 290	− 5.6	3	− 8.7	6	− 16.7	9	− 10.8	6	− 9.1	3
290 to 300	− 5.5	4	+ 4.0	4	− 10.3	8	− 9.8	4	− 13.4	8
300 to 310	− 4.0	4	− 9.5	6	− 9.5	5	− 1.8	1	− 9.1	9
310 to 320	− 8.7	3	− 6.6	5	− 5.6	4	− 3.8	4	− 5.3	6
320 to 330	− 13.3	6	− 4.9	7	− 8.5	5	− 11.3	7	− 1.4	7
330 to 340	− 9.7	4	− 8.8	7	− 8.5	5	− 0.3	8	− 4.3	5
340 to 350	− 3.6	3	− 1.7	4	− 5.1	5	− 9.8	6	+ 8.8	11
350 to 360	− 8.7	8	+ 6.3	4	+ 0.1	6	− 4.0	3	+ 8.5	6
	+136.6	184	+179.5	803	+160.4	195	+ 96.9	155	+ 95.8	800
	−180.6		− 72.8		−118.6		−113.1		−171.0	
	+ 16.0		+106.7		+ 41.8		− 16.2		− 75.8	

Neglecting all terms multiplied by the eccentricity in the coefficients, each residual gives an equation of the form

$$\varDelta l + 2 \sin g\, \varDelta e - 2 \cos g\, e\, \varDelta \varpi = r$$

or, putting

$$h = 2\,\varDelta\delta e = -2\,\delta e$$
$$k = -2\,\varDelta e\,\delta\pi = 2\,e\,\delta\pi$$

the equation will be

$$\varDelta l + h \sin g + k \cos g = r,$$

$\varDelta e$ and $\varDelta\pi$ being the *errors* of the tabular eccentricity and longitude of the perigee, while δe and $\delta\pi$ represent the corresponding *corrections*.

The equations are now solved as if all the residuals within each pair of 20° limits corresponded to the mean of the limit,—that is, as if all between 0° and 20° corresponded to $g = 10°$; those between $g = 20°$ and $g = 40°$ to $g = 30°$; and so on. If, then, we put

$g_1 = 10°$; $g_3 = 30°$, etc.;

r_i, the sum of all the residuals in any one year corresponding to $g = g_i$;

n_i, the corresponding number of observations;

$s_i = \sin g_i$;

$c_i = \cos g_i$:

the normal equations for determining δl, h, and k, by least squares, will be:

$$(\Sigma\,n_i)\ \ \varDelta l + (\Sigma\,n_i\,s_i)\ \ h + (\Sigma\,n_i\,c_i)\ \ k = \Sigma\,r_i$$
$$(\Sigma\,n_i\,s_i)\ \varDelta l + (\Sigma\,n_i\,s_i^2)\ h + (\Sigma\,n_i\,s_i\,c_i)\,k = \Sigma\,s_i\,r_i$$
$$(\Sigma\,n_i\,c_i)\ \varDelta l + (\Sigma\,n_i\,s_i\,c_i)\,h + (\Sigma\,n_i\,c_i^2)\ k = \Sigma\,c_i\,r_i$$

The formation and solution of these equations for each year give the following values of the outstanding errors of the lunar elements for each year:

	$h =$	$k =$
1862,	$+ 0.04$	$+ 1.23$
1863,	$- 0.64$	$+ 1.78$
1864,	$- 1.07$	$+ 1.09$
1865,	$- 1.03$	$- 0.15$
1866,	$- 0.47$	$+ 0.10$
1867,	$- 0.93$	$- 0.36$
1868,	$+ 0.34$	$- 1.46$
1869,	$+ 1.67$	$- 1.56$
1870,	$+ 1.48$	$- 1.14$
1871,	$+ 1.65$	$- 0.36$
1872,	$+ 2.15$	$- 0.12$
1873,	$+ 1.91$	$+ 0.16$
1874,	$+ 1.92$	$+ 0.60$

The periodic character of these residuals is very remarkable, indicating, as it does, either a hitherto unknown inequality of the moon's mean longitude, having nearly the same period with the orbital revolution; or one of the eccentricity and longitude of perigee, having a period of between fifteen and twenty years. To investigate this inequality, we shall assume that each value of h is of the form

$$h - \alpha \sin (\mu + nt)$$

and each value of k of the form

$$k + \alpha' \cos (\mu' + n't),$$

h, k, α, α', μ, μ', n, and n' being unknown quantities to be determined, and t the time in years from any assumed epoch. We shall take for the epoch the middle of the period through which the observations extend; that is, 1868.5. If, then, we represent the thirteen values of h and k in chronological order by h_{-6}, h_{-5} ...., h_0, k_{-6}, k_{-5} ...., k_6, the equations of condition for h and k respectively may be put into the form

$$h_i = h - \alpha \sin \mu \cos i n - \alpha \cos \mu \sin i n$$
$$k_i = k + \alpha' \cos \mu \cos i n - \alpha' \sin \mu \sin i n.$$

Regarding h, k, $\alpha \sin \mu$, $\alpha \cos \mu$, $\alpha' \sin \mu$, and $\alpha' \cos \mu$ as the unknown quantities, the normal equations for determining these quantities are:

(1) *From the values of h_i.*
$$13 h - (\Sigma \cos i n)\, \alpha \sin \mu = \Sigma h_i$$
$$-(\Sigma \cos i n)\, h + (\Sigma \cos^2 i n)\, \alpha \sin \mu = -\Sigma h_i \cos i n$$
$$(\Sigma \sin^2 i n)\, \alpha \cos \mu = -\Sigma h_i \sin i n$$

(2) *From the values of k_i.*
$$13 k + (\Sigma \cos i n)\, \alpha' \cos \mu' = \Sigma k_i$$
$$(\Sigma \cos i n)\, k + (\Sigma \cos^2 i n)\, \alpha' \cos \mu' = \Sigma k_i \cos i n$$
$$\Sigma (\sin^2 i n)\, \alpha' \sin \mu' = -\Sigma k_i \sin i n$$

It will be observed that all the coefficients having as a factor either $\Sigma \sin i n$ or $\Sigma \sin i n \cos i n$ vanish.

The value of n apparently is not readily determined directly by least squares: we shall therefore assume several values of this quantity, and ascertain by which value the conditions can best be satisfied. The following are the abbreviated values of the purely trigonometric summations:

$$\Sigma \cos i n = \frac{\sin 6\frac{1}{2} n}{\sin \frac{1}{2} n} = c$$

$$\Sigma \cos^2 i n = \frac{13 \sin n + \sin 13 n}{2 \sin n} = c_1$$

$$\Sigma \sin^2 i n = \frac{13 \sin n - \sin 13 n}{2 \sin n} = s_1$$

If we solve the preceding equations, and put, for brevity,

$$C = \frac{c}{13\, c_1 - c^2}$$

$$C_1 = \frac{c_1}{13\, c_1 - c^2}$$

$$C_2 = \frac{13}{13\, c_1 - c^2}$$

the resulting expressions for the unknown quantities are:

$$h = C_1 \Sigma h_i - C \Sigma h_i \cos i n$$
$$\alpha \sin \mu = C \Sigma h_i - C_2 \Sigma h_i \cos i n$$
$$\alpha \cos \mu = -\frac{1}{s_1} \Sigma h_i \sin i n$$

$$k = C_1 \Sigma k_i - C \Sigma k_i \cos i n$$
$$\alpha' \cos \mu' = - C \Sigma k_i + C_2 \Sigma k_i \cos i n$$
$$\alpha' \sin \mu' = -\frac{1}{s_1} \Sigma k_i \sin i n$$

The period of h and k lies probably between fifteen and twenty years, which would make the value of n, or the annual motion of the inequality, lie between $18°$ and $24°$. The following are the values of the various quantities depending on n for the different values of n between these limits:

n	$\log \epsilon$	$\log c_1$	$\log s_1$	$\log C$	$\log C$	$\log C_2$
°						
18	0.756	0.715	0.893	9.213	9.172	9.571
19	0.705	0.707	0.898	9.097	9.099	9.506
20	0.644	0.705	0.900	8.977	9.038	9.447
21	0.577	0.709	0.897	8.858	8.990	9.395
22	0.498	0.718	0.891	8.734	8.954	9.350
23	0.406	0.731	0.882	8.604	8.929	9.312
24	0.291	0.747	0.870	8.453	8.909	9.276
25	0.143	0.765	0.856	8.275	8.897	9.246

n	$\Sigma h_i \sin i n$	$\Sigma h_i \cos i n$	$\Sigma k_i \sin i n$	$\Sigma k_i \cos i n$
°	''	''	''	''
18	+ 11.48	+ 1.96	− 4.66	− 4.66
19	+ 11.66	+ 1.52	− 4.68	− 5.04
20	+ 11.78	+ 1.09	− 4.69	− 5.40
21	+ 11.83	+ 0 68	− 4.68	− 5.73
22	+ 11.81	+ 0.29	− 4.66	− 6.04
23	+ 11.73	− 0.08	− 4.62	− 6.33
24	+ 11.58	− 0.44	− 4.57	− 6.60
25	⊢ 11.37	− 0.78	− 4.50	− 6.86

The preceding equations now give the following separate values of the unknown quantities, corresponding to the various assumed values of n:

n	h	a	μ	k	a'	μ'
°	''	''	°	''	''	°
18	0.72	1.53	164.0	0.73	1.81	160.8
19	0.69	1.53	165.2	0.61	1.71	159.7
20	0.66	1.53	166.3	0.49	1.62	158.5
21	0.63	1.54	167.2	0.39	1.53	157.2
22	0.61	1.55	168.1	0.31	1.47	156.0
23	0.60	1.57	169.0	0.23	1.42	154.8
24	0.58	1.59	169.8	0.17	1.39	153.6
25	0.56	1.61	170.4	0.11	1.36	152.6

There can be little serious doubt that in the case of the present inequality the theoretical values of μ and μ' should be the same; and it is also probable that those of α and α' may be substantially identical. The small differences between the values of α and α' and of μ and μ' add so much weight to this probability that we shall make another solution of the equations on the supposition that $\alpha' = \alpha$ and $\mu' = \mu$. The normal equations then become:

$$13\,h - c\alpha \sin \mu = \Sigma h_i$$
$$-c\,h + 13\,\alpha \sin \mu = -\Sigma h_i \cos i\,n - \Sigma k_i \sin i\,n = S_1$$
$$13\,k + c\alpha \cos \mu = \Sigma k_i$$
$$c\,k + 13\,\alpha \cos \mu = \Sigma k_i \cos i\,n - \Sigma h_i \sin i\,n = S_2$$

The solution of these equations is:

$$h = \frac{13}{13^2 - c^2} \Sigma h_i + \frac{c}{13^2 - c^2} S_1$$

$$k = \frac{13}{13^2 - c^2} \Sigma k - \frac{c}{13^2 - c^2} S_2$$

$$\alpha \sin \mu = \frac{13}{13^2 - c^2} S_1 + \frac{c}{13^2 - c^2} \Sigma h_i$$

$$\alpha \cos \mu = \frac{13}{13^2 - c^2} S_2 - \frac{c}{13^2 - c^2} \Sigma k_i$$

A comparison of the separate solutions of the equations in h and k shows that the value of n which best satisfies the conditions lies between $22°$ and $25°$. The values of h, k, α, and μ were therefore derived only from the last equations for the last four values of n. For each of these separate values of n, the corresponding values of h_i and k_i were computed from the formulæ

$$h_i = h - \alpha \sin (\mu + i\,n)$$
$$k_i = k + \alpha \cos (\mu + i\,n)$$

in which, it will be remembered, the index i is simply the number of the year from 1868 ; so that we have,

For 1862, $i = -6$
For 1863, $i = -5$
etc., etc.

These computed values of h_i and k_i were then compared with the values derived directly from observations, and given on page 20, and the sum of the squares of the outstanding residuals was taken. The values of the unknown quantities, together with the sum of the squares of the residuals, are as follow :

n	h	k	α	μ	Σ
°	''	''	''	°	''
22	+ 0.66	+ 0.34	1.54	161.2	3.207
23	+ 0.63	+ 0.27	1.52	161.3	3.170
24	+ 0.61	+ 0.20	1.51	161.5	3.246
25	+ 0.58	+ 0.14	1.49	161.7	3.441

The sum of the squares becomes a minimum for $n = 22°.8$, showing a period of the inequality of $15^y.8$, with a possible error of a year or more. The formulæ for h_i and k_i thus become:

$$h_i = + 0''.64 - 1''.52 \sin (161°.2 + 22°.8\,i)$$
$$k_i = + 0''.28 + 1''.52 \cos (161°.2 + 22°.8\,i)$$

from which we have the following comparison of the computed and observed values of h_i and k_i:

Year.	h_i			k_i		
	C.	O.	O. − C.	C.	O.	O. − C.
	''	''	''	''	''	''
1862	+ 0.01	+ 0.04	+ 0.03	+ 1.67	+ 1.23	− 0.44
1863	− 0.48	− 0.64	0.16	+ 1.32	+ 1.78	+ 0.46
1864	− 0.79	− 1.07	− 0.28	+ 0.80	+ 1.09	+ 0.29
1865	− 0.88	− 1.03	− 0.15	+ 0.22	− 0.15	− 0.37
1866	− 0.74	− 0.47	+ 0.27	− 0.38	+ 0.10	+ 0.48
1867	− 0.37	− 0.93	− 0.56	− 0.85	− 0.36	+ 0.49
1868	+ 0.14	+ 0.34	+ 0.20	− 1.16	− 1.46	− 0.30
1869	+ 0.74	+ 1.67	+ 0.93	− 1.23	− 1.56	− 0.33
1870	+ 1.33	+ 1.48	+ 0.15	− 1.07	− 1.14	− 0.07
1871	+ 1.80	+ 1.65	− 0.15	− 0.70	− 0.36	+ 0.34
1872	+ 2.09	+ 2.15	+ 0.06	− 0.18	− 0.12	+ 0.06
1873	+ 2.15	+ 1.91	− 0.24	+ 0.42	+ 0.16	− 0.26
1874	+ 1.98	+ 1.92	− 0.06	+ 1.00	+ 0.60	− 0.40

The probable residual for each year is $0''.27$.

We have supposed the hypothetical inequality of longitude to be of the form
$$\varDelta v = h_i \sin g + k_i \cos g.$$
Substituting in this the periodic part of h_i and k_i, and replacing i by t, which now represents the time in years from 1868.5, it becomes:
$$\varDelta v = 1''.52 \sin (g + 251°.2 + 22°.8\, t)$$
or
$$\varDelta v = 1''.52 \sin [g + 22°.8\, (Y - 1857.5)]$$

The entirely unexpected character of the periodic term thus brought to light renders its verification by a longer series of observations very desirable. For this purpose, we need comparisons of observations previous to 1862 with Hansen's tables, because none of the older tables with which comparisons have been made are accurate enough for the purpose. Now, the Greenwich Observations for 1859 contain, as an appendix, a comparison of the longitudes and latitudes from Hansen's tables with Greenwich observations from 1847 to 1858 inclusive; and I have utilized the comparison of the longitudes derived from meridian observations in the following way:

A list of limiting dates to tenths of a day was made out, including the whole twelve years, and showing between what dates the moon's mean anomaly was found in each sextant. The sum of the errors in longitude given by the meridian observations was then taken during the period that the anomaly was found in each sextant. None of the corrections found in the first part of this discussion were applied, for the reason that most of them could be treated as accidental errors, and the means could be taken so as nearly to eliminate the effects of the larger ones. A specimen of the form chosen is here given. Under each of the several values of g, given at the tops of the several columns, is shown, firstly, the date at which g had that particular value; and, secondly, the sum of the residuals in longitude during the period of $4^d.6$ between that date and the one next following, together with the number of the residuals, the latter being in small subscript figures.

$g = 0° +$		$g = 60° +$		$g = 120° +$		$g = 180° +$		$g = 240° +$		$g = 300° +$	
1847.	"	1847.	"	1847.	"	1847.	"	1847.	"	1847.	"
Jan. 19.6–	2.9₁	Jan. 24.2–	3.1₁	Jan. 1.2+	1.3₁	Jan. 5.8	..	Jan. 10.4+	8.9₁	Jan. 15.0	..
Feb. 16.1–	1.0₁	Feb. 20.7+	0.4₁	Jan. 26.8+	3.1₁	Feb. 2.4+	3.7₁	Feb. 7.0+	5.6₁	Feb. 11.6	..
Mar. 15.7	..	Mar. 20.3–	3.0₁	Feb. 25.3+	4.5₁	Mar. 1.9+	3.7₁	Mar. 6.5+	2.3₁	Mar. 11.1	..
April 12.3	..	April 16.9	..	Mar. 24.9+	6.1₁	Mar. 24.5–	0.4₁	April 3.1	..	April 7.7+	3.2₁
May 9.8	..	May 14.4	..	April 21.5+	3.2₁	April 26.0+	2.7₁	April 30.6	..	May 5.2+	1.0₁
June 6.2+	2.8₁	June 10.8	..	May 19.0+	2.8₁	May 23.6+	3.5₁	May 26.2–	0.3₁	June 1.8+	4.1₁
July 3.8+	4.4₁	July 8.4	..	June 15.4–	1.4₁	June 20.0–	0.6₁	June 24.6–	2.1₁	June 29.2+	1.9₁
Aug. 0.4–	0.3₁	Aug. 5.0	..	July 13.0	..	July 17.6–	1.6₁	July 22.2+	2.9₁	July 26.8+	6.8₁
Aug. 28.0+	5.9₁	Sept. 1.6+	3.8₁	Aug. 9.6	..	Aug. 14.2	..	Aug. 18.8–	8.4₁	Aug. 23.4+	8.1₁
Sept. 24.6+12.2₂		Sept. 29.2	..	Sept. 6.2	..	Sept. 10.8	..	Sept. 15.4+	3.6₁	Sept. 20.0+	1.0₁
Oct. 22.1+12.2₄		Oct. 26.7+	8.7₁	Oct. 3.8	..	Oct. 8.4	..	Oct. 13.0	..	Oct. 17.6–	7.3₁
Nov. 19.7–	1.2₁	Nov. 23.3+	9.3₁	Oct. 31.3+	1.0₁	Nov. 4.9	..	Nov. 9.5	..	Nov. 14.1	0.0₁
Dec. 16.1–	3.4₁	Dec. 20.7	..	Nov. 27.6+11.4₁		Dec. 2.2	..	Dec. 6.8	..	Dec. 11.4–	1.6₁
				Dec. 25.3+	0.7₁	Dec. 29.9+	0.7₁	Dec. 34.5	..	Dec. 39.1–	2.8₁
1848.		1848.		1848.		1848.		1848.		1848.	
Jan. 12.7–	7.3₁	Jan. 17.3	..	Jan. 21.9	..	Jan. 26.5+	0.2₁	Jan. 31.1	..	Feb. 4.7	..
Feb. 9.3–	8.1₁	Feb. 13.9–	6.2₁	Feb. 18.5–	1.4₁	Feb. 23.1–	1.4₁	Feb. 27.7–	0.8₁	Mar. 3.3	..
Mar. 7.9–	1.8₁	Mar. 12.5–	4.3₁	Mar. 17.1+	4.7₁	Mar. 21.7	..	Mar. 26.3	..	Mar. 30.9	..
April 4.5	..	April 9.1–	4.1₁	April 13.7–	1.5₁	April 18.3–	1.8₁	April 22.9+	2.9₁	April 27.5	..
May 2.0	..	May 6.6–	7.4₁	May 11.2+	1.0₁	May 15.8+	1.4₁	May 20.4+	9.0₁	May 25.0	..
May 29.6	..	June 3.2–	8.9₁	June 7.8–	0.9₁	June 12.4–	0.2₁	June 17.0	..	June 21.6+	2.1₁
June 26.2	..	June 30.8–	2.6₁	July 5.4–	0.6₁	July 10.0–	4.8₁	July 14.6+10.4₁		July 19.2–	0.1₁
July 23.7	..	July 28.3	..	Aug. 1.9–	5.4₁	Aug. 6.5–	3.1₁	Aug. 11.1	..	Aug. 15.7+17.4₁	
Aug. 20.3+	1.2₁	Aug. 24.9	..	Aug. 29.5	..	Sept. 3.1–	6.7₁	Sept. 7.7–	5.1₁	Sept. 12.3+15.7₁	
Sept. 16.9+22.5₁		Sept. 21.5	..	Sept. 26.1	..	Sept. 30.7–	1.0₁	Oct. 5.3+	2.0₁	Oct. 9.8+	8.3₁
Oct. 14.4+	5.1₁	Oct. 19.0	..	Oct. 23.6	..	Oct. 28.2	..	Nov. 1.8+	1.9₁	Nov. 6.4–	4.9₁
Nov. 11.0+	6.9₁	Nov. 15.6+12.8₁		Nov. 20.2	..	Nov. 24.8	..	Nov. 29.4–	9.4₁	Dec. 4.0–	7.8₁
Dec. 8.5–	6.5₁	Dec. 13.1+	5.1₁	Dec. 17.7+	7.0₁	Dec. 22.3	..	Dec. 26.9	..	Dec. 31.5–	5.7₁

If we follow any one of these vertical columns, we shall find that the dates correspond successively to all points of the lunation in a period of 412 days. The first observations of each period will be the last ones of the lunation, and the last ones those made immediately after new moon. Between each pair of periods will be a gap, generally of three or four months, during which the moon was, at the corresponding points of mean anomaly, too near the sun to be observed. If the observations are equally scattered through each period, all the errors arising from erroneous semi-diameter and parallactic inequality will be eliminated. The general minuteness of these errors, and their approach to a balance during each of the periods in question, are such as to render them insignificant, if we take the mean results, not by years, but by periods. This is the course adopted; the partial periods at the beginning and end of the entire series of observations being omitted. The first period actually employed was that corresponding to the sextant 240°–300°, in which the first observation was made on January 10, 1847, and the last on September 18 of the same year. The last period corresponded to the sextant 180°–240°, the last observation in which was on November 13, 1858. There were, in all, ten periods corresponding to each sextant, and hence ten sets of equations, each giving mean values of h, k, and δl for periods extending through a little more than a year. Each residual gave an equation of condition, for the coefficients of which the mean value corresponding to the entire sextant was taken. These values for the several sextants are as follow :

i	g	$\sin g$	$\cos g$	$\sin^2 g$	$\sin g \cos g$	$\cos^2 g$
1	0 – 60	+ 0.48	+ 0.83	0.23	+ 0.40	0.69
2	60 – 120	+ 0.96	0.60	0.91	0.00	0.00
3	120 – 180	+ 0.48	− 0.83	0.23	− 0.40	0.69
4	180 – 240	− 0.48	− 0.83	0.23	+ 0.40	0.69
5	240 – 300	− 0.96	0.00	0.91	0.00	0.00
6	300 – 360	− 0.48	+ 0.83	0.23	− 0.40	0.69

The sums of the residual errors, corresponding to each period and each sextant arranged in chronological order, together with the number of residuals of which each sum is formed, are as follow :

Mean date.	$i = 5$	$i = 6$	$i = 1$	$i = 2$	$i = 3$	$i = 4$
1847.8	+ 6.5	+ 14.4$_{91}$	+ 15.4$_{28}$	− 11.7$_{82}$	+ 9.0$_{81}$	− 16.7$_{17}$
1848.9	+ 6.7	+ 8.7	− 33.0$_{97}$	− 1.9$_{91}$	+ 23.2$_{18}$	+ 31.5$_{17}$
1850.1	+ 1.5	− 34.1$_{17}$	− 40.9$_{83}$	− 9.1$_{88}$	+ 22.2$_{80}$	+ 33.9$_{80}$
1851.2	− 4.5$_{3}$	− 59.4$_{10}$	− 50.7$_{10}$	− 23.5$_{81}$	− 4.8$_{41}$	+ 20.6$_{28}$
1852.4	− 42.8$_{2}$	− 50.0$_{71}$	− 48.0$_{16}$	− 21.5$_{18}$	+ 35.0$_{80}$	+ 25.4$_{12}$
1853.5	− 31.2$_{71}$	− 106.9$_{28}$	− 63.6$_{91}$	+ 1.2$_{17}$	+ 6.0$_{91}$	− 38.0$_{81}$
1854.6	− 30.3$_{17}$	− 94.6$_{84}$	− 35.4$_{83}$	+ 4.2$_{80}$	+ 1.7$_{14}$	− 24.4$_{80}$
1855.8	− 24.3$_{14}$	− 30.0$_{16}$	− 7.3$_{80}$	− 6.9$_{19}$	− 22.8$_{18}$	− 41.0$_{19}$
1856.9	− 36.2	− 23.8$_{14}$	+ 15.4$_{14}$	+ 4.2$_{81}$	− 48.5$_{84}$	− 77.0$_{17}$
1858.1	− 54.9$_{26}$	− 48.9$_{85}$	− 56.7$_{21}$	− 47.6$_{19}$	− 76.9$_{28}$	− 46.2$_{18}$

The dates given in the left-hand column are those corresponding to the mean of each horizontal line.

Putting s_i for the mean value of $\sin g$ corresponding to the index i, as already given; c_i for that of $\cos g$; and n_i for the corresponding number of observations, the normal equations are:

$$n_i \, \Delta l + (\Sigma n_i s_i) \; h + (\Sigma n_i c_i) \; k = \Sigma r_i$$
$$(\Sigma n_i s_i) \, \Delta l + (\Sigma n_i s_i^2) \; h + (\Sigma n_i s_i c_i) \, k = \Sigma s_i r_i$$
$$(\Sigma n_i c_i) \, \Delta l + (\Sigma n_i s_i c_i) \, h + (\Sigma n_i c_i^2) \; k = \Sigma c_i r_i$$

The values of h and k thus given by the normal equations formed from the system of residuals shown in each horizontal line are shown in the next table, which also shows the way in which they are treated. For the sake of completeness, the corresponding quantities already found for the period 1862-74 are added, and included in the discussion, which now proceeds as follows; the method adopted being one which, though less rigorous than the former one, will show in a stronger light the evidence on which the new inequality depends.

As the basis of the discussion, we take the independent values of h and k, derived from each series of observations, which values are given in the second and third columns of the table. A preliminary comparison of the first series of values (1847-58) with the values of h and k derived from the formulæ already given indicates a diminution of the constant terms of those quantities, so that, instead of $+ 0''.64$ and $+ 0''.28$, they become, as a first approximation,

$$h_0 = + 0''.50$$
$$k_0 = + 0''.10$$

These constants are now subtracted from the values of h and k, leaving a series of residuals given in the fourth and fifth columns, which, if the periodic term under investigation has no existence, should be regarded as due to errors of observation, and, in the contrary case, should be representable by the formulæ

$$h' = - \alpha \sin (\mu + nt) + \text{accidental errors}$$
$$k' = \alpha \cos (\mu + nt) + \text{accidental errors}$$

To show clearly how far they are thus represented, we determine a coefficient, α, and an angle, N, by the equations

$$\alpha \sin N = - h'$$
$$\alpha \cos N = k'$$

The next two columns give the several values of α and N thus obtained. The nearly regular progression of the angle N is too striking to be overlooked. To see how nearly this angle can be represented as one increasing uniformly with the time, we solve the necessary equations of condition by least squares. It is obvious that the greater the value of α the more certain will be the value of N: we therefore give weights proportional to α. Moreover, weights nearly twice as great in proportion are given to the second series (1862-74) as containing the results from two observatories, and being more carefully corrected. The values of μ and n thus obtained by the method of least squares are:

$$\mu = 164°.6 \pm 4°.4$$
$$n = 20.8 \pm 0.47$$

The probable error of a value of N of weight unity comes out

$$\pm 33°$$

The residuals still outstanding are shown in the column ΔN. This value of n is 2° less than that found from the second series of observations alone, and an examination of the residuals shows that there is a real discordance between the values of the angular motion of N given by the two series. It is quite likely that the relative weights assigned to the older series of observations are twice as great as they should be, and that the most probable value of the angle N lies nearly half-way between the two values

$$161°.2 + 22°.8 (t - 1868.5)$$

and

$$164°.6 + 20°.8 (t - 1868.5)$$

found from the last series alone, and from the two combined. I judge that the most probable value is

$$N = 163°.2 + 21°.6 (t - 1868.5),$$

and that the probable error of the annual motion is more than half a degree, but less than a degree. The column $\Delta'N$ shows the residuals given by this value of N.

Mean date.	h	k	h'	k'	a	N	Wt.	$\mu + nt$	ΔN	$\Delta'N$
	"	"	"	"	"	°		°	°	°
1847.6	− 0.08	+ 0.55	− 0.58	+ 0.45	0.74	52	1	94	+ 42	+ 24
1848.9	− 0.55	− 1.38	− 1.05	− 1.48	1.82	145	3	118	− 27	− 44
1850.1	− 0.20	− 1.91	− 0.70	− 2.01	2.13	161	3	141	− 20	− 36
1851.2	− 0.32	− 1.92	− 0.82	− 2.02	2.18	158	3	165	+ 7	− 8
1852.4	+ 0.26	− 2.45	− 0.24	− 2.55	2.56	175	4	189	+ 14	0
1853.5	+ 1.10	− 1.88	+ 0.60	− 1.98	2.07	197	3	212	+ 15	+ 2
1854.6	+ 1.45	− 1.40	+ 0.95	− 1.50	1.77	212	3	236	+ 24	+ 12
1855.8	+ 0.77	+ 0.31	+ 0.27	+ 0.21	0.34	308	¼	260	− 48	− 60
1856.9	+ 1.76	+ 1.82	+ 1.26	+ 1.72	2.13	328	3	284	− 44	− 55
1858.1	− 0.17	+ 0.66	− 0.67	+ 0.56	0.88	50	1	307	−103	−112
1862.5	+ 0.04	+ 1.23	− 0.46	+ 1.13	1.22	22	3	40	+ 18	+ 12
1863.5	− 0.64	+ 1.78	− 1.14	+ 1.68	2.03	34	5	61	+ 27	+ 21
1864.5	− 1.07	+ 1.09	− 1.57	+ 0.99	1.85	58	5	81	+ 23	+ 19
1865.5	− 1.03	− 0.15	− 1.53	− 0.25	1.55	99	4	102	+ 3	− 1
1866.5	− 0.47	+ 0.10	− 0.97	0.00	0.97	90	2	123	+ 33	+ 30
1867.5	− 0.93	− 0.36	− 1.43	− 0.46	1.50	108	4	144	+ 36	+ 34
1868.5	+ 0.34	− 1.46	− 0.16	− 1.56	1.57	174	4	165	− 9	− 11
1869.5	+ 1.67	− 1.56	+ 1.17	− 1.66	2.03	215	5	185	− 30	− 30
1870.5	+ 1.48	− 1.14	+ 0.98	− 1.24	1.58	218	5	206	− 12	− 12
1871.5	+ 1.65	− 0.36	+ 1.15	− 0.46	1.24	248	3	227	− 21	− 20
1872.5	+ 2.15	− 0.12	+ 1.65	− 0.22	1.66	262	4	248	− 14	− 12
1873.5	+ 1.91	+ 0.16	+ 1.41	+ 0.06	1.41	272	4	269	− 3	− 1
1874.5	+ 1.92	+ 0.60	+ 1.42	+ 0.50	1.50	289	4	289	0	+ 4

The old and new series of observations agree well in giving for the value of the coefficient of this term,

The old series, $a = 1''.66$
The new series, $a = 1''.55$

The effect of the accidental errors will be, on the whole, to increase the value of the coefficient. I consider therefore that the value

$$a = 1''.50$$

may be adopted as the most probable which can be derived from all the observations.

If we subtract, from each value of h and k in the preceding table, the periodic portions

$$h' = -1''.50 \sin [163°.2 + 21°.6 (t - 1868.5)]$$
$$k' = 1''.50 \cos [163°.2 + 21°.6 (t - 1868.5)]$$

and take the mean value of the outstanding remainder for each series of observations we find it to be as follows:

Old series, $h_0 = +0''.33$; $k_0 = -0''.17$
New series, $h_0 = +0''.65$; $k_0 = +0''.36$

The differences, $0''.01$ and $0''.08$, between these last values and those found on page 23 arise from the different value of the periodic term. I consider that the results of the second series are entitled to three times the weight of those of the first, and shall therefore put for the definitive values of h and k,

$$h = +0''.57 + h'$$
$$k = +0''.23 + k'$$

The corresponding corrections to the eccentricity and longitude of perigee are:

$$\delta e = -0''.29$$
$$e \, \delta\pi = +0''.12$$
$$\delta\pi = +2''.2$$

The corrections to the moon's longitude are:

$$\delta l = -h \sin g - k \cos g$$
$$= -0''.57 \sin g - 0''.23 \cos g + 1''.50 \sin (g + N - 90°).$$

The last term is the hitherto-unsuspected inequality indicated by observations, but not yet known to be given by theory. It may be either an inequality of the eccentricity and perigee having a period of about 16⅔ years, or one of the moon's mean longitude having a period of

$$27^d.4304 \pm 0^d.0040$$

Substituting first for N, and then for g, their values in terms of the time, the expression for the inequality of longitude becomes

$$1''.50 \sin [g + 73°.2 + 21°.6 (t - 1868.5)] = 1''.50 \sin (56°.8 + 13°.12413 \, \tau),$$

τ being the time in days counted from Greenwich mean noon of 1850, Jan. 0.

It would perhaps be premature to introduce so purely empirical a term as this into lunar tables for permanent use; but where, as at present, it is requisite to obtain the corrections to the tables during a limited period with all possible accuracy, the evidence in favor of the reality of the term seems strong enough to justify its introduction. The only apparent cause to which the term can be attributed is the attraction of some one of the planets.

In the investigation of corrections to the longitude, it only remains to determine the slowly-varying corrections to the mean longitude, or to $n \, \delta z$, given by the observations. To determine the errors of short period, we have applied several corrections to the residuals, not as real, but only to render the various observations comparable. We have now to consider the pure results of observations as they would have been had these corrections not been applied. These for the second series of observations are found by taking the sum of (1) the mean of the small corrections, applied on account of observatory and limb, to compensate for the systematic differences between results from different limbs or different observatories; (2) general corrections to make the residuals in the mean very small; (3) remaining outstanding correction found by solving the equations of condition.

The corrections from both series are as follow: the corrections since 1862 may be very closely represented by a term increasing uniformly with the time, as is shown by the last two columns.

First series.

Date.	n dz	Date.	n dz
	''		''
1847.8	− 0.15	1853.5	+ 1.77
1848.9	− 0.43	1854.6	+ 1.40
1850.1	+ 0.32	1855.8	+ 1.24
1851.2	+ 1.13	1856.9	+ 1.50
1852.4	+ 0.93	1858.1	+ 2.40

Second series.

Year.	(1)	(2)	(3)	n dz	a + bt	Δ
	''	''	''	''	''	''
1862.5	+ 0.45	+ 2.10	+ 0.04	+ 2.59	+ 1.52	+ 1.07
1863.5	+ 0.45	+ 1.20	− 0.27	+ 1.38	+ 0.60	+ 0.78
1864.5	0.00	0.00	− 0.49	− 0.49	− 0.32	− 0.17
1865.5	− 0.15	− 1.15	− 0.62	− 1.92	− 1.24	− 0.68
1866.5	− 0.15	− 2.00	− 0.75	− 2.90	− 2.16	− 0.74
1867.5	− 0.15	− 3.40	− 0.41	− 3.96	− 3.08	− 0.88
1868.5	− 0.15	− 4.05	− 0.20	− 4.40	− 4.00	− 0.40
1869.5	+ 0.08	− 4.85	− 0.21	− 4.98	− 4.92	− 0.06
1870.5	+ 0.08	− 5.50	− 0.09	− 5.51	− 5.84	+ 0.33
1871.5	0.00	− 6.35	− 0.52	− 6.87	− 6.76	− 0.11
1872.5	− 0.15	− 7.25	− 0.22	− 7.62	− 7.68	+ 0.06
1873.5	0.00	− 8.30	+ 0.10	− 8.20	− 8.60	+ 0.40
1874.5	0.00	− 9.45	+ 0.38	− 9.07	− 9.52	+ 0.45

§ 2.

INVESTIGATION OF THE POLAR DISTANCE AND LATITUDE.

It is a singular circumstance that during the last six years, at least, the observations of the moon's polar distance are much less accurate than those of its right ascension. Whether this is to be attributed to the instruments, or whether it is a result of great irregularities in the outline of the lunar globe in the polar regions, cannot at present be decided. To whatever cause we attribute the errors, their existence renders a rigorous treatment of the individual observations of little value. We shall therefore, from the whole of the errors in declination, seek to obtain the best corrections to the inclination and node of the moon's orbit.

From the derivatives of the moon's declination relatively to its true longitude, the inclination, and the node, which have already been given, we obtain:

$$\delta\delta = \frac{d\delta}{dl}\,\delta l + \frac{d\delta}{d\theta}\,\delta\theta + \frac{d\delta}{di}\,\delta i$$

δl being known from the data already given, the equations of condition will be thrown into the form

$$\frac{d\delta}{i\,d\theta}\,i\,\delta\theta + \frac{d\delta}{di}\,\delta i = \delta\delta - \frac{d\delta}{dl}\,\delta l$$

From the numerical expressions already given, we have

$$\frac{d\delta}{dl}\,\delta l = \sec\delta\left[(0.40 + 0.08\cos\theta)\cos l + 0.08\sin\theta\sin l\right]\delta l$$

If we put

$\delta\lambda =$ the correction to the moon's mean longitude,
$K = 0.40 + 0.08\cos\theta$,
$H = 0.08\sin\theta$,

we have the quantities of the first order, with respect to the eccentricities,

$$\frac{d\delta}{d\lambda} = [K\cos l + H\sin l]\,[1 + 2\,e\cos(\lambda - \pi)]\sec\delta$$

The largest terms in sec δ are

$$1.040 + .016\cos\theta - .040\cos 2\lambda - .016\cos(2\lambda - \theta),$$

while, if we replace l by the mean longitude, λ, we shall have:

$$l = \lambda + 2\,e\sin(\lambda - \pi)$$
$$\sin l = \sin\lambda + e\sin(2\lambda - \pi) - e\sin\pi$$
$$\cos l = \cos\lambda + e\cos(2\lambda - \pi) - e\cos\pi$$

If we substitute these various quantities in the expression for $\frac{d\delta}{dl}\,\delta l$, we shall find no sensible terms depending on the sine or cosine of the argument of latitude, $\lambda - \theta$. If we substitute for δl its value in $\delta \lambda$, we shall find the principal terms in $\cos \delta \frac{d\delta}{dl} \frac{dl}{d\lambda}$ to be

$$K \cos \lambda + H \sin \lambda + 3 e K \cos (2 \lambda - \pi) + 3 e H \sin (2 \lambda - \pi)$$

In consequence of the great number of revolutions of the moon through which the observations now under discussion extend, I have considered that all except the first two terms might be treated as accidental errors, which would cancel each other during the course of the observations. Using for $\delta \lambda$ the mean corrections to the moon's longitude, we have the following values of the correction to the declination for those errors of longitude:

Year.	Correction.
1862,	$+ 0.9 \cos l - 0.2 \sin l$
1863,	$+ 0.6 \qquad - 0.1$
1864,	$- 0.1 \qquad 0.0$
1865,	$- 0.6 \qquad + 0.1$
1866,	$- 0.8 \qquad 0.0$
1867,	$- 0.1 \qquad - 0.1$
1868,	$- 1.4 \qquad - 0.2$
1869,	$- 1.8 \qquad - 0.3$
1870,	$- 2.2 \qquad - 0.4$
1871,	$- 2.8 \qquad - 0.6$
1872,	$- 3.3 \qquad - 0.6$
1873,	$- 3.8 \qquad - 0.5$
1874,	$- 4.2 \qquad - 0.4$

The mean correction to the moon's tabular north-polar distance for each year, from observations of each limb at each observatory, was taken with a view of detecting any constant error of sufficient magnitude to affect the final results for errors of the node and inclination. These means should have been taken after the application of the corrections just found: actually, however, they are the mean corrections given by the observations, after applying the following constant corrections to reduce the declinations to the same fundamental standard:

To Greenwich observations of N. P. D.	To Washington observations of N. P. D.
1862–67, $- 0.4$	1862–65, $+ 0.5$
1868–74, $+ 0.2$	1866–67, $- 1.1$
	1868, $\quad - 1.2$
	1869, $\quad - 0.6$
	1870–72, $- 0.4$
	1873–74, $\quad 0.0$

These corrections are approximately those necessary to reduce the star-observations of the several years to Auwers's standard of declination. The change in the Greenwich correction between 1867 and 1868 probably arises from the introduction of a new constant of refraction in 1868, while the change in the Washington correction in 1866 corresponds to the introduction of the large transit circle in place of the old mural circle.

Year.	Correction to N. P. D. gives by—			
	Greenwich.		Washington.	
	N. L.	S. L.	N. L.	S. L.
	"	"	"	"
1862	− 0.1	− 0.8	− 0.3	− 0.8
1863	+ 0.8	− 0.9	− 0.5	− 1.1
1864	+ 0.4	− 0.6	+ 0.8	− 0.9
1865	+ 0.5	− 0.8	+ 1.8	− 0.8
1866	− 0.7	− 0.3	+ 1.4	− 0.6
1867	− 0.4	− 0.6	+ 0.1	− 1.1
1868	− 0.7	− 1.0	+ 0.9	+ 0.8
1869	− 0.1	− 0.6	− 0.8	− 1.7
1870	− 0.6	− 0.1	− 0.1	− 1.8
1871	− 0.8	− 0.8	+ 8.1	− 1.8
1872	0.0	0.0	− 0.7	− 0.8
1873	− 0.9	+ 0.1	+ 8.0	− 0.1
1874	. .	. .	− 1.7	− 0.5

The large residuals of the Washington observations of the south limb led to the application of the farther systematic correction of + 1".0 to all those observations before combining them all. The corrections arising from the error of mean longitude were then applied, and the outstanding residuals were considered to arise from accidental errors and from errors of the inclination and node. The equations of condition thus become

$$0.92 \sec \delta \left[\sin (l - \theta) \, \delta i - \cos (l - \theta) \, i \, \delta \theta \right] = \delta \delta$$

or

$$\sin (l - \theta) \, \delta i - \cos (l - \theta) \, i \, \delta \theta = 1.09 \cos \delta \times \delta \delta$$

Owing to the smallness of the final residuals, $\delta \delta$, the factor $1.09 \cos \delta$ may be considered as a constant, and, in the actual solution, has been put equal to unity. Its mean value is more exactly 1.04, and its effect may be obtained by dividing the final results by this factor.

The final values of the residuals were then arranged according to the values of $\lambda - \theta$, or the moon's mean argument of latitude, as the residuals in right ascension were arranged according to the mean anomaly. The sum of the residuals corresponding to each interval of 20° in the argument, with the corresponding number of observations for each year, is shown in the following table:

5 M

Sums of errors of the moon's corrected declination, given by observations at Greenwich and Washington.

Limits of λ.	1862.		1863.		1864.		1865.		1866.		1867.		1868.	
	Σδδ	N.	Σδδ	N.	Σδδ	N.	Σδδ	N.	Σδδ	N.	Σδδ	N.	Σδδ	N.
° °	"		"		"		"		"		"		"	
0 to 20	− 3.8	8	+ 1.3	3	+ 4.0	8	+ 5.4	9	+26.7	11	− 2.5	8	+ 0.4	9
20 to 40	+ 9.6	9	+ 5.8	7	− 0.4	9	+ 6.0	7	+ 2.6	12	− 2.3	9	− 6.1	17
40 to 60	− 1.4	9	+ 6.9	10	+ 6.5	6	+ 9.7	7	+ 4.0	9	− 4.9	10	− 7.9	15
60 to 80	0.0	7	+16.4	10	+ 6.6	8	+ 8.7	12	− 1.1	16	+14.5	11	− 0.3	5
80 to 100	+ 8.6	11	+ 0.4	12	+11.1	6	+ 7.9	11	+ 5.5	7	+ 0.5	10	−12.8	12
100 to 120	+ 3.2	7	+ 8.5	15	+ 3.2	5	+ 7.4	7	− 1.0	8	− 6.1	6	+ 0.2	6
120 to 140	− 9.2	12	+ 3.1	8	− 6.1	8	+ 0.8	11	+11.9	14	−12.4	8	− 6.8	11
140 to 160	− 0.3	4	− 4.6	9	− 2.2	5	− 9.7	15	− 1.2	10	− 7.7	12	+ 6.2	14
160 to 180	+ 0.5	9	−10.4	6	−10.4	12	+ 0.5	9	+ 2.2	10	− 8.9	9	−11.2	9
180 to 200	− 8.6	6	− 5.7	11	− 0.6	7	− 5.3	12	− 7.7	6	−15.2	14	+ 3.1	10
200 to 220	−22.3	8	−11.6	10	+ 4.7	12	− 5.4	9	− 3.3	10	− 6.8	14	−11.8	11
220 to 240	−14.4	12	−10.2	9	− 8.8	10	− 1.0	7	− 2.0	13	− 5.9	12	−10.0	13
240 to 260	−12.4	7	−12.3	9	− 4.1	8	+ 4.6	11	+ 1.2	9	− 0.6	9	− 9.2	15
260 to 280	− 2.3	4	− 3.2	4	− 8.5	8	+ 1.5	9	− 5.3	9	+ 1.0	8	+ 1.9	9
280 to 300	− 2.2	7	− 4.3	8	− 8.4	11	− 4.0	4	− 3.5	9	−11.4	13	0.0	13
300 to 320	− 7.1	10	− 6.2	10	+ 9.6	8	+ 3.1	5	− 0.1	13	− 8.4	10	+ 0.4	8
320 to 340	+ 2.0	7	+ 3.4	8	+ 6.0	12	+ 8.6	6	+ 8.4	11	+ 2.1	9	− 6.7	14
340 to 360	+ 7.3	5	− 6.5	5	+ 4.9	13	+11.6	8	+ 7.0	14	+ 2.9	3	− 3.1	12
	−84.0	142	−75.0	154	−49.5	156	−25.4	159	−25.2	191	−93.1	175	−85.9	203
	+31.2		+45.8		+56.6		+75.8		+69.5		+21.0		+12.2	
	−52.8		−29.2		+ 7.1		+50.4		+44.3		−72.1		−73.7	

Sums of errors of the moon's corrected declination, &c.—Continued.

Limits of λ	1869.		1870.		1871.		1872.		1873.		1874.	
	ΣΔd	N.	ΣΔd	N.	ΣΔd	N.	ΣΔd	N.	ΣΔd	N.	ΣΔd	N.
0 to 20	+ 7.1	8	+ 3.7	7	− 3.8	5	− 8.0	6	+ 9.0	9	+ 7.7	12
20 to 40	+ 11.8	8	+ 6.6	10	− 0.1	4	− 7.0	6	− 7.7	10	− 7.5	7
40 to 60	+ 6.4	7	+ 8.6	10	− 0.5	11	− 1.8	10	− 8.8	4	− 17.0	11
60 to 80	− 5.0	9	+ 3.5	7	+13.8	11	− 5.1	7	−13.7	7	− 25.4	14
80 to 100	− 8.0	11	+ 6.8	9	+13.1	9	− 3.7	8	+ 4.8	9	− 5.3	6
100 to 120	− 13.7	7	− 6.8	12	− 6.3	9	− 8.0	8	− 1.0	9	− 28.4	12
120 to 140	− 11.4	9	+ 4.5	7	− 1.9	8	+ 0.8	14	− 8.8	4	+ 8.1	6
140 to 160	− 15.4	18	−11.7	11	− 4.6	7	− 8.9	9	+ 7.4	5	− 12.6	11
160 to 180	− 8.5	11	− 5.7	13	− 5.1	9	− 4.6	12	− 3.9	7	− 5.9	10
180 to 200	− 5.4	9	− 0.5	6	+ 5.4	11	− 6.0	3	− 8.6	7	− 7.8	8
200 to 220	− 5.4	4	−10.8	12	− 6.8	10	− 8.9	9	+ 5.8	7	− 19.3	12
220 to 240	− 6.6	6	− 1.1	9	+ 9.1	14	− 4.5	10	− 8.7	5	− 15.8	6
240 to 260	− 18.4	18	−11.1	8	+ 5.6	8	+15.7	13	+14.8	18	− 4.6	6
260 to 280	− 7.7	7	−15.4	15	− 6.8	7	+ 8.8	11	+80.7	9	− 8.5	6
280 to 300	− 11.4	13	−10.1	5	+ 3.6	8	+ 3.8	9	+ 3.3	10	− 5.5	13
300 to 320	+ 5.3	7	− 9.1	7	+ 3.8	8	− 1.3	11	+ 4.3	8	+ 0.3	10
320 to 340	+ 5.7	5	−10.3	12	− 5.8	9	−18.8	12	+14.0	7	+ 4.0	10
340 to 360	0.0	10	− 1.2	6	− 6.3	5	+ 0.3	9	+ 7.8	11	− 3.9	9
	−104.9	155	−92.6	166	−47.1	153	−67.4	167	−43.6	140	−154.3	169
	+ 35.7		+33.1		+53.8		+20.2		+90.7		+ 14.1	
	− 69.2		−59.5		+ 6.7		−47.2		+48.1		−140.2	

The general irregularity of the residuals in declination is such that no great advantage would result in a separate solution of the equations for the separate years. The sum of the residuals for each 20° of the argument was therefore taken during the whole thirteen years of observation, with the following result:

λ − θ	ΣΔd	N.	λ − θ	ΣΔd	N.
0 to 20	+ 47.8	103	180 to 200	− 68.3	110
20 to 40	+ 10.7	115	200 to 220	− 95.3	128
40 to 60	+ 6.1	119	220 to 240	− 73.3	126
60 to 80	+ 12.3	124	240 to 260	− 38.8	127
80 to 100	+ 34.3	121	260 to 280	− 83.8	106
100 to 120	− 36.8	111	280 to 300	− 50.1	123
120 to 140	− 87.4	120	300 to 320	− 5.4	115
140 to 160	− 69.3	124	320 to 340	+ 19.8	122
160 to 180	− 65.4	126	340 to 360	+ 80.8	110

Leaving in the equations a constant term δp, representing the mean constant error still outstanding in the measures of declination, the solution of the equations of condition given by the residuals gives the following results:

$$\varDelta p = -0''.17$$
$$\varDelta i = +0''.15$$
$$i \varDelta \theta = -0''.40$$

or,

Correction to the inclination, $-0''.15$

Correction to the longitude of node, $+4''.5$

This correction to the longitude of the node from Hansen's tables implies a diminution of the secular retrograde motion of the node, which is quite accordant with the results derived from ancient eclipses. Hansen remarks that an increase of $12''$ per century in the longitude of the moon's node will improve the agreement of his tables with ancient eclipses;[*] and, if we suppose the tabular longitude of the node to have been correct in 1825, this would imply a correction of $+5''.2$ to the longitude of the node in 1868.

---

[*] Darlegung, etc., Th. ii, p. 391.

§ 3.

AUXILIARY TABLES FOR FACILITATING THE COMPUTATION OF THE CORREC-
TIONS TO HANSEN'S "TABLES DE LA LUNE", GIVEN BY THE PRECEDING DIS-
CUSSION.

The following is a summary of the corrections to the longitude of the moon from
Hansen's tables given by the preceding discussion. The first six terms are applicable
to the disturbed mean longitude, or "*Argument fondamental*"; the remainder to the
true longitude; but they may all be used as corrections of the "*Argument fondamental*"
without serious error:

Corrections on account of diminution of the solar parallax .. $n \, \delta z = + 0''.96 \sin D$
$$+ 0''.07 \sin (D - g)$$
$$- 0''.13 \sin (D + g')$$

On account of hypothesis (here provisionally set aside), that
the moon's center of gravity does not coincide with the
center of figure, together with the correction to the evec-
tion resulting from the correction to the eccentricity ... $n \, \delta z = + 0''.09 \sin g'$
$$- 0''.33 \sin 2 D$$
$$- 0''.21 \sin (2 D - g)$$

On account of term accidentally introduced into
the tables with a wrong sign .... $\delta v = - 0''.62 \sin (2 g - 4 g' + 2 \omega - 4 \omega')$

On account of correction to the eccentricity and perigee
found from observations during 1847-74 .... $\delta v = - 0''.57 \sin g - 0''.23 \cos g$
$$= \quad 0''.62 \sin (g + 202°.0)$$

Empirical term, necessary to satisfy observations,
but not verified by theory .... $+ 1''.50 \sin [g + 21°.6 (Y - 1865.1)]$

Unexplained correction to the mean longitude, changing slowly from year to
year .... See Table IV.

The deduction of all these terms, except the last, has been fully given in the preceding pages. This secular correction to the mean longitude has been derived from the
outstanding errors of mean longitude given on page 30, in the column $n \, \delta z$, by suppos-
ing this quantity to vary according to some simple law, which law changes when necessary,
so as to satisfy the observations within the mean limits of their probable error. An
examination of Table IV shows, that, from 1848.0 to 1855.5, the correction is supposed
to increase uniformly at the rate of 0''.20 per annum. It is then supposed to remain
constant until nearly 1863.0, a period during which the observations are not continuous,
there being no comparisons with theory from 1859 to 1861 inclusive. From 1863.0
until the present time, the observations are well represented by the correction
$$- 5''.53 - 0''.86 (t - 1870.0) + 0''.02 (t - 1870.0)^2$$
The continuance of this correction beyond 1875.0 is, of course, purely conjectural.

TABLES FOR APPLYING THE PRECEDING CORRECTIONS.

The following tables are designed to facilitate the computation of the corrections just given. To avoid the necessity of referring to Hansen's tables, the values of all the necessary arguments are given for the years 1850 to 1889 in Tables I to III.

Table I: the epochs are January 0, Greenwich mean noon of common years, and January 1 of leap years. All the arguments increase uniformly by a unit in a day.

Argument g is the moon's mean anomaly, converted into days by dividing its expression in degrees by 13.065. It is equal to Hansen's argument g diminished by 15 days.

Argument D shows the number of days since mean new moon, or, it is the mean departure of the moon from the sun expressed in days. It is equal to Hansen's argument 33 diminished by 30 days, or, which amounts to the same thing, by $0^d.47$.

Argument A gives the number of days from the time when the angle

$$2 g - 4 g' + 2 \omega - 4 \omega'$$

was last zero.

Argument B is that of the empirical term indicated by observations, but not given by theory.

Argument u is that of latitude, or the number of days since the mean moon last passed her ascending node.

Tables II and III do not seem to need explanation. In using the former, care must be taken to diminish by one day the dates for January and February of leap years.

Table IV gives the secular corrections to the mean longitude, or to $n\delta z$, obtained from observations in the manner already described.

Table V, argument A, gives the correction for the term introduced into the tables with a wrong sign, described on page 9. It is properly to be applied to the true longitude, and is therefore designated as δv.

Table VI gives the empirical term, which, so far as is known, may be applied to the true longitude.

Table VII gives the sum of the terms of mean longitude

$$+ 0''.96 \sin D$$
$$- 0''.33 \sin 2 D$$
$$- 0''.13 \sin (D + g')$$
$$+ 0''.09 \sin g'$$

The sun's mean anomaly, g', having a period of a year, the sum of these terms can be expressed as a function of D and the month, and is given in the table for the middle of each month, and for each day of D.

Table VIII gives the sum of the terms of true longitude which depend wholly or partly on the moon's mean anomaly, namely:

$$+ 0''.62 \sin (g + 202°.0)$$
$$+ 0''.07 \sin (D - g)$$
$$- 0''.21 \sin (2 D - g)$$

The sum of the terms of $n \, \delta z$ are to be reduced to corrections of the longitude in orbit by multiplication by the factor

$$1 + 2 e \cos g + \frac{5}{2} e^2 \cos 2 g_j$$

This factor, less unity, is given in Table IX.

For convenience, the unit of the factor is omitted from the tabular numbers, so that it is only necessary to add the product $F \times n \, \delta z$ in with $n \, \delta z$ and δv to have the correction of the true longitude in orbit.

These corrections being applied to the longitude of the moon's center from Hansen's tables, that longitude may be regarded as correct, excepting a small correction, which may probably be regarded as constant during any one period not exceeding six months, and which may be attributed to the adopted position of the equinox. It will be best determined from occultations of stars observed at points whose longitudes from Greenwich are accurately known by telegraph, and will then be applicable to the determination of the longitude of any station from occultations.

If the corrections here deduced are applied to the errors of the lunar ephemeris derived from meridian observations, it must be remembered that these observations are made on the moon's limb, while the corrections are applicable to the center. Hence, the value of the moon's semi-diameter must, if great refinement is aimed at, be varied with the observer, the instrument, and the brightness of the sky. For large instruments, Hansen's semi-diameter is about $1''$ too great, even at night.

The sum of all the terms of $n \, \delta z$, δv, and $F \times n \, dz$ from the tables will be the correction of the longitude in orbit. This will not be rigorously the same as the correction to the ecliptic longitude.

Table X gives the small factor $(F. l)$ by which the orbit longitude must be increased or diminished to obtain the ecliptic longitude. This factor may generally be disregarded.

Table X also gives the data for the correction of the moon's latitude, namely, (1) a factor $(F. \beta)$ by which the correction of the moon's argument of latitude must be multiplied; and (2) the term

$$\delta\beta_1 = -0''.15 \sin u$$

arising from the correction to the tabular inclination of the moon's orbit. The correction of the moon's argument of latitude being that of her longitude, *minus* the correction of her node, the whole correction to the latitude will be

$$\delta\beta = \delta\beta_1 + (F. \beta)\,(\delta v - 4''.5)$$

Table XI gives the factors for converting corrections of longitude and latitude into corrections of right ascension and declination. The formulæ are

$$\delta . \mathcal{R} = \delta v + (v.\,\alpha)\,\delta v + (\beta.\,\alpha)\,\delta\beta$$
$$\delta . \mathrm{Dec.} = \delta\beta + (v.\,\delta)\,\delta v + (\beta.\,\delta)\,\delta\beta$$

The side argument is the moon's longitude, and in the coefficients $(v.\,\alpha)$ and perhaps $(\beta.\,\alpha)$ regard must be had to the moon's latitude also. Three columns are therefore given for latitude, $-5°$, $0°$, and $+5°$ respectively.

As an example of the use of the tables of corrections, we will commence the determination of the corrections for September, 1874. We find the values of the arguments for September 1, from Tables I to III, as follows:

	g	*D*	*A*	*B*	*u*
1874 . . .	5.4	12.1	8.0	20.0	1.9
Sept. 1 . .	23.6	7.8	1.9	24.6	26.2
Periods . .	−27.6	. .	. .	−27.4	−27.2
Arg. Sept. 1 .	1.4	19.9	9.9	17.2	0.9
Arg. Oct. 1 .	3.8	20.3	39.9 or 7.8	47.2 or 19.8	30.9 or 3.7

$$D = 19.9$$
$$g = 1.4$$
$$D - g = 18.5$$

The tabular numbers are then found as follows, with an argument increasing by unity each day. From Table VIII, we take a mean from columns 18 and 19.

September . .	1.	2.	3.	4.	5.	6.	7.	8.
Table IV (*n ds*) .	− 9.11	− 9.11	− 9.11	− 9.11	− 9.12	− 9.12	− 9.12	− 9.12
V (*dv*) .	+ 0.40	+ 0.55	+ 0.62	+ 0 59	+ 0.48	+ 0.28	+ 0.05	− 0.18
VI (*dv*) .	− 1.07	− 1.29	− 1.42	− 1.50	− 1.48	− 1.40	− 1.23	− 1.01
VII (*n ds*) .	− 1.29	− 1.25	− 1.12	− 0.95	− 0.76	− 0.56	− 0.37	− 0.22
VIII (*dv*) .	− 0.65	− 0.72	− 0.77	− 0.78	− 0.75	− 0.69	− 0.60	− 0.48
	−11.72	−11.82	−11.80	−11.75	−11.63	−11.49	−11.27	−11.01
n ds × *F*, Table IX	− 1.12	− 0.93	− 0.71	− 0.47	− 0.28	− 0.06	+ 0.18	+ 0.37
dv	−12.84	−12.75	−12.51	−12.22	−11.91	−11.55	−11.09	−10.64
dv − 4″.5 . . .	−17.3	−17.2	−17.0	−16.7	−16.4	−16.0	−15.6	−15.1
Table X (*F . β*) .	+ 0.088	+ 0.082	+ 0.070	+ 0.056	+ 0.038	+ 0.019	− 0.002	− 0.022
X (*δ β₁*) .	− 0.03	− 0.07	− 0.10	− 0.12	− 0.14	− 0.15	− 0.15	− 0.14
(*dv* − 4″.5)(*F. β*) .	− 1.52	− 1.38	− 1.19	− 0.93	− 0.63	− 0.30	+ 0.03	+ 0.33
δβ	− 1.55	− 1.45	− 1.29	− 1.05	− 0.77	− 0.45	− 0.12	+ 0.19
☾'s longitude .	46.5	60.7	74.6	88.1	101.5	114.5	127.4	140.0
(1 +(*v . α*)) *dv* .	−13.08	−13.49	−13.84	−13.81	−13.39	−12.61	−11.62	−10.67
(*β.α*) *δβ* . . .	+ 0.47	+ 0.32	+ 0.16	+ 0.02	− 0.07	− 0.09	− 0.03	+ 0.06
dR . . . . {	−12.6 / − 0″.84	−13.2 / − 0″.88	−13.7 / − 0″.91	−13.8 / − 0″.92	−13.5 / − 0″.90	−12.7 / − 0″.85	−11.6 / − 0″.78	−10.6 / − 0″.71
(*v . δ*) *dv* . . .	− 3.70	− 2.64	− 1.41	− 0.18	+ 1.02	+ 2.05	+ 2.84	+ 3.35
(1 + *β.δ*) *δβ* . .	− 1.50	− 1.42	− 1.28	− 1.05	− 0.77	− 0.44	− 0.12	+ 0.18
δDec.	− 5.2	− 4.1	− 2.7	− 1.2	+ 0.2	+ 1.6	+ 2.7	+ 3.5

41

This computation has been continued to 1875, January 31, and the results are shown in the following table:

Corrections to the Ephemeris derived from Hansen's Tables of the Moon, for Greenwich mean noon of each day, from 1874, September 1, to 1875, January 31.

Date. Gr. mean noon.	Correction to tabular—				Date. Gr. mean noon.	Correction to tabular—			
	Long.	Lat.	R. A.	Dec.		Long.	Lat.	R. A.	Dec.
1874. Sept. 1	−12.8	−1.6	−12.6	−5.8	1874. Oct. 11	−7.5	+1.1	−6.7	+3.6
2	12.8	1.5	13.8	4.1	12	7.8	1.0	6.8	3.8
3	12.5	1.3	13.7	8.7	13	6.9	1.0	6.8	8.7
4	12.3	1.0	13.8	−1.8	14	6.6	0.8	7.0	8.0
5	11.9	0.8	13.5	+0.8	15	6.4	0.7	7.0	1.3
6	−11.6	−0.5	−12.7	+1.6	16	−6.8	+0.5	−7.0	+0.6
7	11.1	−0.1	11.6	8.7	17	6.1	0.3	6.9	−0.8
8	10.6	+0.8	10.6	3.5	18	6.8	+0.1	6.8	1.0
9	10.1	0.5	9.6	4.1	19	6.4	−0.1	6.6	1.8
10	9.6	0.7	8.6	4.3	20	6.8	0.4	6.6	8.5
11	−9.0	+0.9	−7.9	+4.4	21	−7.5	−0.6	−6.9	−3.3
12	8.3	1.0	7.3	4.8	22	8.3	0.9	7.3	4.1
13	7.6	1.1	6.7	3.8	23	9.3	1.1	8.1	4.7
14	6.8	1.0	6.8	3.3	24	10.4	1.3	9.8	5.8
15	6.8	1.0	5.9	8.8	25	11.4	1.5	10.6	5.8
16	−5.6	+0.9	−5.7	+8.8	26	−18.4	−1.5	−18.8	−4.8
17	5.8	0.7	5.5	1.6	27	13.8	1.4	13.9	3.8
18	5.0	0.6	5.5	1.0	28	13.6	1.8	15.1	8.3
19	5.1	0.4	5.8	+0.3	29	13.8	1.0	15.7	−0.6
20	5.4	+0.8	6.1	−0.4	30	13.6	0.6	15.3	+1.1
21	−6.1	0.0	−6.6	−1.8	31	−13.8	−0.3	−14.8	+8.6
22	7.0	−0.8	7.8	8.8	Nov. 1	18.4	+0.1	18.6	3.6
23	8.1	0.5	7.8	3.8	2	11.4	0.4	11.1	4.3
24	9.4	0.8	8.5	4.3	3	10.5	0.7	9.6	4.5
25	10.6	1.1	9.3	5.8	4	9.5	0.8	8.4	4.5
26	−11.8	−1.3	−10.3	−5.8	5	−8.5	+1.0	−7.4	+4.3
27	18.7	1.5	11.5	6.0	6	7.7	1.0	6.7	3.9
28	13.4	1.6	18.8	5.7	7	7.1	1.0	6.3	3.5
29	13.7	1.5	13.9	4.8	8	6.6	1.0	6.8	3.1
30	13.8	1.4	14.9	3.4	9	6.4	1.0	6.8	8.6
Oct. 1	−13.5	−1.8	−15.8	−1.7	10	−6.3	+0.9	−6.5	+8.1
2	13.0	0.9	14.7	−0.1	11	6.3	0.7	6.9	1.5
3	12.8	0.5	13.6	+1.4	12	6.5	0.6	7.3	+0.8
4	11.5	−0.8	18.8	8.6	13	6.8	0.4	7.7	−0.1
5	10.6	+0.1	10.8	3.3	14	7.1	+0.1	7.8	1.0
6	−9.9	+0.4	−9.4	+3.9	15	−7.4	−0.1	−7.8	−1.8
7	9.8	0.6	8.4	4.1	16	7.7	0.4	7.7	8.7
8	8.7	0.8	7.7	4.8	17	8.1	0.6	7.6	3.4
9	8.8	1.0	7.8	4.8	18	8.4	0.8	7.6	4.0
10	7.8	1.0	6.8	4.0	19	8.9	1.0	7.8	4.5

6 ×

Corrections to the Ephemeris derived from Hansen's Tables of the Moon, etc.—Continued.

Date. Gr. mean noon.	Correction to tabular—				Date. Gr. mean noon.	Correction to tabular—			
	Long.	Lat.	R.A.	Dec.		Long.	Lat.	R.A.	Dec.
1874.	"	"	"	"	1874.	"	"	"	"
Nov. 20	− 9.4	− 1.2	− 8.2	− 4.8	Dec. 27	− 10.8	+ 0.6	− 10.2	+ 4.3
21	10.0	1.3	9.0	4.8	28	10.4	0.8	9.5	4.7
22	10.6	1.3	10.1	4.5	29	10.1	1.0	8.9	4.9
23	11.2	1.3	11.4	3.8	30	9.6	1.2	8.4	4.9
24	11.7	1.2	12.7	2.6	31	9.2	1.2	8.1	4.6
25	− 12.2	− 1.0	− 13.8	− 1.2	1875.				
26	12.5	0.6	14.1	+ 0.5	Jan. 1	− 8.7	+ 1.2	− 7.9	+ 4.1
27	12.6	− 0.3	13.8	2.0	2	8.2	1.1	7.9	3.5
28	12.5	0.0	13.0	3.3	3	7.8	1.0	7.9	2.9
29	12.1	+ 0.4	11.9	4.3	4	7.4	0.9	7.9	2.1
30	− 11.7	+ 0.7	− 10.9	+ 4.9	5	7.1	0.6	7.8	1.2
Dec. 1	11.0	0.9	9.9	5.1	6	− 6.9	+ 0.4	− 7.8	+ 0.4
2	10.3	1.1	9.0	5.1	7	6.8	+ 0.2	7.7	− 0.5
3	9.4	1.2	8.2	4.7	8	6.9	0.0	7.5	1.4
4	8.5	1.2	7.5	4.2	9	7.2	− 0.3	7.4	2.2
5	− 7.7	+ 1.1	− 7.0	+ 3.6	10	7.6	0.5	7.3	3.0
6	7.0	1.0	6.8	3.0	11	− 8.0	− 0.7	− 7.3	− 3.7
7	6.4	0.9	6.6	2.3	12	8.6	1.0	7.5	4.3
8	6.1	0.8	6.5	1.6	13	9.2	1.2	8.0	4.7
9	6.0	0.6	6.7	0.9	14	9.7	1.3	8.6	4.9
10	− 6.1	+ 0.4	− 6.9	+ 0.1	15	10.3	1.4	9.5	4.8
11	6.4	+ 0.2	7.1	− 0.7	16	− 10.8	− 1.3	− 10.6	− 4.3
12	6.8	0.0	7.3	1.5	17	11.2	1.2	11.7	3.4
13	7.4	− 0.3	7.5	2.4	18	11.5	1.0	12.6	2.2
14	8.0	0.6	7.6	3.3	19	11.6	0.8	13.1	− 0.8
15	− 8.7	− 0.8	− 7.8	− 4.0	20	11.6	0.5	13.0	+ 0.8
16	9.3	1.1	8.1	4.7	21	− 11.5	− 0.1	− 12.4	+ 2.2
17	9.9	1.2	8.6	5.0	22	11.1	+ 0.2	11.4	3.3
18	10.3	1.3	9.2	5.1	23	10.7	0.5	10.3	4.1
19	10.7	1.4	10.0	4.8	24	10.2	0.7	9.3	4.5
20	− 11.0	− 1.3	− 11.0	− 4.1	25	9.6	1.0	8.5	4.6
21	11.2	1.2	12.0	3.1	26	− 9.1	+ 1.1	− 7.9	+ 4.6
22	11.4	1.0	12.7	1.7	27	8.5	1.1	7.5	4.3
23	11.4	0.7	12.9	− 0.2	28	8.1	1.1	7.2	4.0
24	11.4	0.4	12.6	+ 1.3	29	7.7	1.1	7.2	3.5
25	− 11.3	− 0.1	− 12.0	+ 2.6	30	7.5	1.0	7.4	2.9
26	11.1	+ 0.3	11.1	3.6	31	− 7.4	+ 0.9	− 7.7	+ 2.3

TABLES.

TABLES.

TABLE I.	TABLE II.
Values of the Arguments for the beginning of each year.	*Reduction of the Arguments to the zero-day of each month.*

Year.	ε	D	A	B	ϖ		Month.	ε	D	A	B	ϖ
1850	1.8	16.7	6.3	4.3	25.5		Jan. 0°	0.0	0.0	0.0	0.0	0.0
1851	8.6	27.3	0.0	12.7	9.5		Feb. 0°	3.4	1.5	14.9	3.6	3.8
1852 B	16.4	9.4	10.9	22.1	21.7		Mar. 0	3.9	0.0	10.6	4.1	4.6
1853	23.1	20.0	4.7	3.1	5.8		April 0	7.3	1.4	9.3	7.7	8.4
1854	2.4	1.1	14.6	11.5	17.0		May 0	9.8	1.9	7.0	10.3	11.8
1855	9.2	11.8	8.4	19.9	1.0		June 0	13.2	3.3	5.7	13.8	14.9
1856 B	17.0	23.4	3.2	1.9	13.3		July 0	15.7	3.8	3.5	16.4	17.7
1857	23.8	4.5	13.1	10.3	24.5		Aug. 0	19.1	5.3	2.8	20.0	21.5
1858	3.0	15.1	6.9	18.7	8.5		Sept. 0	22.6	6.8	0.9	23.6	25.2
1859	9.8	25.8	0.7	27.1	19.8		Oct. 0	25.0	7.2	14.8	26.1	0.9
1860 B	17.6	7.9	11.6	9.1	4.8		Nov. 0	0.9	8.7	13.5	2.3	4.7
1861	24.4	18.5	5.3	17.5	16.0		Dec. 0	3.3	9.1	11.2	4.8	7.5
1862	3.6	29.2	15.2	25.9	0.1							
1863	10.4	10.2	9.0	6.9	11.3		*In January and February of leap-years,
1864 B	18.2	21.9	3.7	16.3	23.6		the numbers taken from Table II are to be
1865	25.0	3.0	13.7	24.7	7.6		diminished by a unit.
1866	4.2	13.6	7.4	5.7	18.8		
1867	11.0	24.3	1.2	14.1	2.8		### TABLE III.
1868 B	18.8	6.4	12.1	23.5	15.1		
1869	25.6	17.0	5.9	4.4	26.3		*Periods of the Arguments.*
1870	4.8	27.6	15.8	12.8	10.4		
1871	11.6	8.7	9.6	21.3	21.6			ε	D	A	B	ϖ
1872 B	19.4	20.4	4.4	3.2	6.6							
1873	26.2	1.5	14.3	11.6	17.9		P . .	27.6	29.5	16.1	27.4	27.8
1874	5.4	12.1	8.0	20.0	1.9		2 P . .	55.1	59.1	32.3	54.9	54.4
1875	12.2	22.7	1.8	1.0	13.1		3 P . .	82.7	88.6	48.4	82.3	81.6
1876 B	20.0	4.8	12.7	10.4	25.4		4 P . .	110.2	118.1	64.6	109.7	108.8
1877	26.8	15.5	6.5	18.8	9.4							
1878	6.0	26.1	0.3	27.2	20.7		
1879	12.8	7.2	10.2	8.2	4.7		
1880 B	20.6	18.8	5.0	17.6	16.9		
1881	27.4	29.4	14.9	26.0	1.0		
1882	6.6	10.6	8.6	7.0	12.2		
1883	13.4	21.2	2.4	15.4	23.4		
1884 B	21.2	3.3	13.3	24.8	8.5		
1885	0.5	13.9	7.1	5.8	19.7		
1886	7.3	24.6	0.9	14.2	3.7		
1887	14.0	5.7	10.8	22.6	15.0		
1888 B	21.8	17.3	5.5	4.6	0.0		
1889	28.6	27.9	15.4	13.0	11.2		

TABLE IV.
Secular Terms.

Year.	n dt	Diff.
1848.0	0.00	
1849.0	+ 0.20	+ 0.20
1850.0	0.40	0.20
1851.0	0.60	0.20
1852.0	0.80	0.20
1853.0	1.00	0.20
1854.0	+ 1.20	+ 0.20
1855.0	1 40	0.20
1856.0	1.50	+ 0.10
1857.0	1.50	0.00
1858.0	1.50	0.00
1859.0	+ 1.50	0.00
1860.0	1.50	0.00
1861.0	1.50	0.00
1862.0	1.50	— 0.03
1863.0	1.47	— 1.12
1864.0	+ 0.35	— 1.08
1865.0	— 0.73	— 1.04
1866.0	— 1.77	— 1.00
1867.0	— 2.77	— 0.96
1868.0	— 3.73	— 0.92
1869.0	— 4.65	— 0.88
1870.0	— 5.53	— 0.84
1871.0	— 6.37	— 0.80
1872.0	— 7.17	— 0.76
1873.0	— 7.93	— 0.72
1874.0	— 8.65	— 0.68
1875.0	— 9.33	— 0.64
1876.0	— 9.97	— 0.60
1877.0	— 10.57	— 0.56
1878.0	— 11.13	— 0.52
1879.0	— 11.65	— 0.48
1880.0	— 12.13	

TABLE V.
Argument A.

A	δv
0	0.00
1	— 0.23
2	— 0.44
3	— 0.57
4	— 0.62
5	— 0.57
6	— 0.44
7	— 0.25
8	— 0.02
9	+ 0.22
10	0.42
11	0.56
12	0.62
13	0.58
14	+ 0.46
15	0.26
16	+ 0.03
17	— 0.20
18	— 0.42
19	— 0.56
20	— 0.62
21	— 0.59
22	— 0.47
23	— 0.28
24	— 0.05
25	+ 0.19
26	0.40
27	0.55
28	0.62
29	0.59
30	+ 0.49
31	0.30
32	+ 0.07
33	— 0.17
34	— 0.38
35	— 0.54
36	— 0.62
37	— 0.60
38	— 0.49
39	— 0.31
40	— 0.09
41	+ 0.15
42	0.38
43	0.54
44	0.61
45	0.60
46	+ 0.51
47	0.33
48	+ 0.10
49	— 0.14
50	— 0.36

TABLE VI.
Argument B (Empirical Term).

B	δv	B	δv
0	0.00	40	+ 0.39
1	+ 0.34	41	+ 0.05
2	0.66	42	— 0.29
3	0.95	43	— 0 62
4	1.19	44	— 0.91
5	+ 1.37	45	— 1.16
6	1.47	46	— 1.34
7	1.50	47	— 1.46
8	1.45	48	— 1.50
9	1.32	49	— 1.46
10	+ 1.13	50	— 1.34
11	0.88	51	— 1.16
12	0.57	52	— 0.91
13	+ 0.25	53	— 0.62
14	— 0.10	54	— 0.29
15	— 0.44	55	+ 0.05
16	— 0.75	56	0.39
17	— 1.03	57	0.71
18	— 1.25	58	0.99
19	— 1.40	59	1.22
20	— 1.49	60	+ 1.39
21	— 1.49	61	1.48
22	— 1.42	62	1.50
23	— 1.27	63	1.44
24	— 1.06	64	1.30
25	— 0.79	65	+ 1.08
26	— 0.48	66	0.83
27	— 0.15	67	0.53
28	+ 0.19	68	+ 0.19
29	0.53	69	— 0.15
30	+ 0.83	70	— 0.48
31	1.08	71	— 0.79
32	1.30	72	— 1.06
33	1.44	73	— 1.27
34	1.50	74	— 1.42
35	+ 1.48	75	— 1.49
36	1.39	76	— 1.49
37	1.22	77	— 1.40
38	0.99	78	— 1.25
39	0.71	79	— 1.03
40	+ 0.39	80	— 0.75

Table VII, $\pi\,\delta s$.

Arguments, D and the month.

D	Jan.	Feb.	Mar.	April.	May.	June	July.	Aug.	Sept.	Oct.	Nov.	Dec.
0	−0.01	−0.03	−0.04	−0.04	−0.03	−0.01	+0.01	+0.03	+0.04	+0.04	+0.03	+0.01
1	+0.05	+0.01	+0.02	+0.03	+0.05	+0.08	+0.10	+0.11	+0.11	+0.10	+0.07	+0.05
2	0.08	0.09	0.10	0.13	0.16	0.19	0.21	0.20	0.19	0.16	0.13	0.10
3	0.16	0.19	0.22	0.26	0.29	0.32	0.34	0.31	0.28	0.24	0.21	0.18
4	0.29	0.32	0.38	0.43	0.46	0.49	0.49	0.46	0.41	0.36	0.32	0.29
5	+0.45	+0.50	+0.56	+0.62	+0.66	+0.67	+0.67	+0.62	+0.56	+0.50	+0.46	+0.45
6	0.63	0.68	0.77	0.83	0.85	0.87	0.85	0.79	0.71	0.65	0.62	0.60
7	0.80	0.87	0.96	1.03	1.05	1.06	1.02	0.95	0.86	0.80	0.77	0.76
8	0.93	1.02	1.12	1.18	1.20	1.19	1.15	1.06	0.96	0.90	0.88	0.89
9	1.02	1.12	1.21	1.27	1.29	1.27	1.21	1.11	1.01	0.95	0.94	0.96
10	+1.04	+1.15	+1.25	+1.30	+1.30	+1.26	+1.18	+1.08	+0.98	+0.93	+0.93	+0.97
11	0.97	1.07	1.18	1.22	1.20	1.15	1.07	0.96	0.86	0.82	0.83	0.89
12	0.82	0.92	1.03	1.06	1.02	0.96	0.86	0.76	0.66	0.63	0.66	0.72
13	0.58	0.62	0.77	0.79	0.74	0.66	0.56	0.46	0.37	0.35	0.40	0.48
14	+0.28	0.39	0.47	0.48	0.42	+0.32	+0.22	+0.12	+0.04	+0.03	+0.09	+0.18
15	−0.02	+0.08	+0.14	+0.14	+0.07	−0.03	−0.13	−0.23	−0.30	−0.30	−0.22	−0.12
16	−0.34	−0.25	−0.20	−0.22	−0.29	−0.40	−0.50	−0.59	−0.64	−0.68	−0.55	−0.44
17	−0.60	−0.53	−0.49	−0.52	−0.61	−0.71	−0.81	−0.89	−0.92	−0.89	−0.81	−0.70
18	−0.81	−0.74	−0.72	−0.76	−0.86	−0.97	−1.05	−1.12	−1.14	−1.00	−1.00	−0.89
19	−0.93	−0.88	−0.88	−0.89	−1.02	−1.13	−1.21	−1.26	−1.23	−1.22	−1.18	−1.01
20	−0.97	−0.94	−0.94	−1.00	−1.10	−1.21	−1.27	−1.30	−1.30	−1.24	−1.14	−1.03
21	−0.95	−0.92	−0.93	−0.99	−1.09	−1.18	−1.24	−1.25	−1.23	−1.17	−1.08	−0.99
22	−0.83	−0.83	−0.86	−0.92	−1.01	−1.09	−1.13	−1.13	−1.10	−1.04	−0.95	−0.87
23	−0.69	−0.70	−0.72	−0.78	−0.87	−0.94	−0.96	−0.95	−0.92	−0.86	−0.78	−0.67
24	−0.51	−0.54	−0.59	−0.64	−0.71	−0.77	−0.79	−0.77	−0.73	−0.67	−0.60	−0.55
25	−0.37	−0.39	−0.43	−0.48	−0.54	−0.59	−0.59	−0.56	−0.52	−0.47	−0.41	−0.37
26	−0.23	−0.27	−0.31	−0.36	−0.40	−0.41	−0.41	−0.35	−0.34	−0.29	−0.25	−0.23
27	−0.14	−0.17	−0.20	−0.24	−0.27	−0.28	−0.26	−0.23	−0.20	−0.16	−0.13	−0.12
28	−0.07	−0.11	−0.12	−0.15	−0.16	−0.16	−0.14	−0.10	−0.09	−0.06	−0.05	−0.05
29	−0.03	−0.06	−0.07	−0.08	−0.06	−0.06	−0.04	−0.02	0.00	+0.01	0.00	−0.01
30	0.00	−0.01	−0.02	−0.01	0.00	+0.02	+0.04	+0.06	+0.07	0.06	+0.05	+0.02
31	+0.05	+0.05	+0.07	+0.06	+0.10	0.13	0.15	0.16	0.14	0.13	0.11	0.07
32	+0.11	+0.14	+0.16	+0.19	+0.22	+0.26	+0.27	+0.26	+0.23	+0.20	+0.17	+0.14

Note.—Each column is computed for the middle of the month, but may be used for the entire month without an error ever exceeding 0."05. If much greater accuracy than this is required, a horizontal interpolation must be used.

TABLE VIII, δv.

Horizontal Argument, or Argument at top, D−g, or D−g+30. Vertical Argument, g.

g	0	1	2	3	4	5	6	7	8	9	10	11	12	13	14
0	−0.23	−0.30	−0.36	−0.39	−0.39	−0.35	−0.28	−0.19	−0.11	−0.03	+0.02	+0.03	0.00	−0.06	−0.15
1	−0.39	−0.46	−0.50	−0.53	−0.50	−0.44	−0.36	−0.28	−0.19	−0.12	−0.09	−0.09	−0.14	−0.22	−0.31
2	−0.54	−0.60	−0.64	−0.62	−0.58	−0.52	−0.43	−0.34	−0.25	−0.20	−0.19	−0.21	−0.27	−0.35	−0.45
3	−0.66	−0.71	−0.72	−0.69	−0.64	−0.56	−0.47	−0.37	−0.31	−0.27	−0.26	−0.31	−0.38	−0.47	−0.58
4	−0.75	−0.77	−0.77	−0.74	−0.67	−0.58	−0.48	−0.39	−0.34	−0.31	−0.33	−0.38	−0.46	−0.57	−0.67
5	−0.79	−0.81	−0.80	−0.74	−0.66	−0.55	−0.46	−0.39	−0.34	−0.34	−0.36	−0.43	−0.53	−0.64	−0.74
6	−0.80	−0.81	−0.76	−0.70	−0.60	−0.50	−0.42	−0.35	−0.33	−0.33	−0.38	−0.47	−0.57	−0.67	−0.76
7	−0.78	−0.76	−0.71	−0.62	−0.52	−0.43	−0.34	−0.30	−0.28	−0.31	−0.38	−0.47	−0.57	−0.67	−0.73
8	−0.71	−0.68	−0.61	−0.51	−0.42	−0.32	−0.26	−0.22	−0.22	−0.27	−0.35	−0.45	−0.54	−0.61	−0.68
9	−0.62	−0.56	−0.47	−0.38	−0.28	−0.20	−0.14	−0.12	−0.15	−0.21	−0.30	−0.38	−0.47	−0.53	−0.58
10	−0.49	−0.41	−0.33	−0.22	−0.13	−0.06	−0.02	−0.02	−0.06	−0.13	−0.22	−0.30	−0.37	−0.44	−0.48
11	−0.33	−0.26	−0.16	−0.06	+0.03	+0.09	+0.11	+0.10	+0.04	−0.03	−0.12	−0.19	−0.28	−0.33	−0.33
12	−0.18	−0.08	+0.02	+0.11	0.19	0.24	0.25	0.21	0.15	+0.07	−0.01	−0.10	−0.17	−0.18	−0.18
13	0.00	+0.10	0.19	0.28	0.35	0.38	0.37	0.33	0.26	0.19	+0.09	0.00	−0.03	−0.04	−0.01
14	+0.17	0.26	0.36	0.45	0.50	0.51	0.49	0.41	0.37	0.27	0.17	+0.13	+0.10	+0.11	+0.14
15	+0.32	+0.42	+0.52	+0.59	+0.63	+0.62	+0.59	+0.53	+0.43	+0.34	+0.28	+0.23	+0.23	+0.24	+0.29
16	0.46	0.56	0.65	0.71	0.73	0.71	0.66	0.58	0.48	0.42	0.35	0.33	0.33	0.37	0.43
17	0.58	0.68	0.75	0.80	0.79	0.76	0.68	0.60	0.53	0.46	0.42	0.41	0.43	0.48	0.56
18	0.67	0.76	0.82	0.84	0.82	0.77	0.69	0.62	0.54	0.49	0.46	0.47	0.50	0.57	0.65
19	0.73	0.80	0.83	0.84	0.81	0.75	0.67	0.59	0.53	0.48	0.48	0.49	0.56	0.63	0.72
20	+0.74	+0.79	+0.81	+0.80	+0.76	+0.69	+0.61	+0.54	+0.49	+0.47	+0.46	+0.51	+0.58	+0.67	+0.73
21	0.70	0.75	0.76	+0.73	0.67	0.60	0.53	0.47	0.43	0.41	0.41	0.51	0.58	0.65	0.71
22	0.64	0.67	0.67	+0.62	0.56	0.48	0.42	0.37	0.33	0.35	0.40	0.47	0.53	0.60	0.67
23	0.55	0.57	0.54	+0.49	0.42	0.35	0.29	0.24	0.21	0.27	0.33	0.38	0.48	0.55	0.60
24	0.45	0.43	0.39	+0.33	0.26	0.20	+0.13	+0.12	0.13	0.17	0.22	0.31	0.40	0.46	0.50
25	+0.29	+0.28	+0.22	+0.16	+0.10	+0.02	−0.01	−0.02	+0.01	+0.05	+0.14	+0.24	+0.31	+0.36	+0.37
26	+0.15	+0.11	+0.06	−0.01	−0.09	−0.14	−0.16	−0.16	−0.13	−0.04	+0.06	0.13	0.20	0.23	0.23
27	0.02	−0.06	−0.12	−0.20	−0.26	−0.30	−0.31	−0.30	−0.22	−0.13	−0.04	+0.04	+0.08	+0.10	+0.08
28	−0.17	−0.22	−0.30	−0.37	−0.42	−0.46	−0.46	−0.39	−0.31	−0.22	−0.13	−0.07	−0.02	−0.03	−0.07
29	−0.31	−0.38	−0.46	−0.52	−0.57	−0.59	−0.54	−0.47	−0.39	−0.29	−0.22	−0.15	−0.13	−0.15	−0.20
30	−0.45	−0.52	−0.60	−0.66	−0.69	−0.66	−0.60	−0.54	−0.44	−0.36	−0.27	−0.23	−0.23	−0.26	−0.32

TABLE VIII, δv—Continued.

Horizontal Argument, or Argument at top, $D-g$, or $D-g+30$.   Vertical Argument, g.

g	15	16	17	18	19	20	21	22	23	24	25	26	27	28	29	30
0	−0.25	−0.35	−0.43	−0.48	−0.48	−0.46	−0.40	−0.31	−0.23	−0.14	−0.04	−0.07	−0.08	−0.12	−0.18	−0.26
1	−0.41	−0.51	−0.58	−0.61	−0.61	−0.51	−0.48	−0.40	−0.30	−0.23	−0.20	−0.20	−0.23	−0.28	−0.35	−0.48
2	−0.56	−0.64	−0.69	−0.71	−0.68	−0.62	−0.55	−0.45	−0.39	−0.33	−0.31	−0.32	−0.36	−0.42	−0.54	−0.67
3	−0.68	−0.74	−0.79	−0.78	−0.74	−0.67	−0.56	−0.51	−0.44	−0.40	−0.39	−0.42	−0.47	−0.55	−0.63	−0.70
4	−0.76	−0.82	−0.83	−0.81	−0.76	−0.67	−0.60	−0.52	−0.47	−0.45	−0.41	−0.50	−0.57	−0.65	−0.73	−0.77
5	−0.81	−0.84	−0.84	−0.80	−0.74	−0.66	−0.58	−0.52	−0.48	−0.48	−0.50	−0.56	−0.64	−0.72	−0.78	−0.80
6	−0.80	−0.83	−0.81	−0.76	−0.69	−0.62	−0.54	−0.44	−0.47	−0.47	−0.52	−0.60	−0.68	−0.74	−0.78	−0.81
7	−0.77	−0.77	−0.74	−0.68	−0.60	−0.53	−0.47	−0.43	−0.42	−0.46	−0.52	−0.60	−0.67	−0.73	−0.77	−0.77
8	−0.64	−0.64	−0.61	−0.57	−0.50	−0.43	−0.39	−0.35	−0.37	−0.42	−0.50	−0.57	−0.63	−0.69	−0.71	−0.70
9	−0.60	−0.56	−0.51	−0.43	−0.37	−0.31	−0.26	−0.28	−0.30	−0.34	−0.43	−0.51	−0.58	−0.62	−0.62	−0.59
10	−0.46	−0.42	−0.35	−0.28	−0.22	−0.16	−0.14	−0.16	−0.21	−0.27	−0.35	−0.43	−0.49	−0.52	−0.51	−0.45
11	−0.30	−0.25	−0.19	−0.12	−0.04	−0.01	−0.02	−0.04	−0.10	−0.18	−0.27	−0.34	−0.39	−0.40	−0.36	−0.29
12	−0.13	−0.08	−0.01	+0.07	+0.13	+0.19	+2.18	+0.08	0.00	−0.09	−0.17	−0.23	−0.26	−0.25	−0.20	−0.13
13	+0.03	+0.10	+0.18	0.24	0.27	0.28	0.25	0.18	+0.10	+0.01	−0.08	−0.12	−0.13	−0.10	−0.03	+0.05
14	0.20	0.28	0.35	0.40	0.43	0.41	0.35	0.28	0.19	0.10	+0.03	0.00	+0.01	+0.05	+0.12	0.22
15	+0.37	+0.44	+0.51	+0.55	+0.55	+0.51	+0.44	+0.35	+0.26	+0.18	+0.13	+0.11	+0.13	+0.19	+0.28	+0.36
16	0.51	0.58	0.65	0.66	0.63	0.58	0.50	0.41	0.33	0.25	0.21	0.21	0.25	0.31	0.40	0.51
17	0.63	0.71	0.74	0.73	0.69	0.63	0.54	0.45	0.36	0.30	0.28	0.29	0.35	0.42	0.52	0.63
18	0.73	0.76	0.78	0.77	0.72	0.64	0.55	0.45	0.38	0.33	0.33	0.36	0.41	0.51	0.60	0.71
19	0.77	0.80	0.81	0.78	0.71	0.62	0.52	0.43	0.37	0.34	0.35	0.39	0.47	0.57	0.66	0.76
20	+0.77	+0.80	+0.79	+0.74	+0.66	+0.56	+0.46	+0.39	+0.34	+0.34	+0.36	+0.42	+0.50	+0.60	+0.70	+0.77
21	0.76	0.76	0.73	0.67	0.57	0.47	0.39	0.31	0.28	0.28	0.32	0.39	0.46	0.56	0.68	0.73
22	0.70	0.68	0.64	0.55	0.45	0.36	0.28	0.23	0.20	0.22	0.28	0.37	0.46	0.55	0.69	0.66
23	0.60	0.58	0.51	0.42	0.32	0.23	0.16	+0.11	0.11	0.15	0.22	0.30	0.40	0.48	0.53	0.57
24	0.40	0.43	0.35	0.26	+0.18	+0.06	+0.07	−0.01	+0.01	+0.06	0.14	0.23	0.31	0.38	0.43	0.44
25	+0.34	+0.27	+0.19	+0.07	0.00	−0.07	−0.13	−0.12	−0.11	−0.05	+0.03	+0.12	+0.20	+0.27	+0.31	+0.29
26	0.18	+0.11	+0.01	−0.08	−0.17	−0.24	−0.27	−0.26	−0.23	−0.15	−0.07	+0.03	+0.10	+0.14	+0.15	+0.12
27	+0.02	−0.06	−0.16	−0.25	−0.31	−0.39	−0.41	−0.39	−0.33	−0.26	−0.16	−0.08	−0.02	0.00	−0.01	−0.05
28	−0.14	−0.23	−0.32	−0.42	−0.49	−0.53	−0.54	−0.50	−0.43	−0.35	−0.25	−0.19	−0.14	−0.11	−0.17	−0.20
29	−0.28	−0.37	−0.48	−0.57	−0.63	−0.65	−0.64	−0.58	−0.50	−0.41	−0.34	−0.28	−0.26	−0.27	−0.29	−0.35
30	−0.41	−0.51	−0.62	−0.69	−0.73	−0.74	−0.70	−0.64	−0.55	−0.47	−0.41	−0.37	−0.37	−0.37	−0.42	−0.49

7 M

TABLE IX.		TABLE X.			
Argument, g. Factor to be multiplied by n δz.		*Argument, u. Factors for correction of latitude and reduction to ecliptic longitude.*			
g	F	u	(F,l)	(F,β)	$\delta\beta_1$
					''
0	+ 0.118	0	− 0.004	+ 0.090	0.00
1	0.114	1	− 0.004	0.088	− 0.03
2	0.103	2	− 0.003	0.081	− 0.07
3	0.086	3	− 0.001	0.069	− 0.10
4	0.065	4	+ 0.001	0.054	− 0.12
5	+ 0.040	5	+ 0.003	+ 0.036	− 0.14
6	+ 0.015	6	0.004	+ 0.017	− 0.15
7	− 0.009	7	0.004	− 0.004	− 0.15
8	− 0.034	8	0.004	− 0.024	− 0.14
9	− 0.054	9	+ 0.002	− 0.044	− 0.13
10	− 0.072	10	0.000	− 0.060	− 0.11
11	− 0.086	11	− 0.001	− 0.074	− 0.08
12	− 0.096	12	− 0.003	− 0.084	− 0.05
13	− 0.101	13	− 0.004	− 0.089	− 0.02
14	− 0.103	14	− 0.004	− 0.089	+ 0.01
15	− 0.099	15	− 0.003	− 0.085	+ 0.05
16	− 0.092	16	− 0.002	− 0.076	0.08
17	− 0.080	17	0.000	− 0.064	0.11
18	− 0.065	18	+ 0.002	− 0.047	0.13
19	− 0.046	19	0.003	− 0.028	0.14
20	− 0.024	20	+ 0.004	− 0.008	+ 0.15
21	+ 0.001	21	0.004	+ 0.012	0.15
22	0.026	22	0.003	0.032	0.14
23	0.051	23	+ 0.001	0.050	0.12
24	0.075	24	0.000	0.066	0.10
25	+ 0.094	25	− 0.002	+ 0.078	+ 0.07
26	0.109	26	− 0.004	0.086	0.04
27	0.116	27	− 0.004	0.090	+ 0.01
28	0.117	28	− 0.004	0.089	− 0.03
29	0.110	29	− 0.003	0.082	− 0.06
30	+ 0.096	30	− 0.001	+ 0.072	− 0.09

TABLE XI.

Factors for converting small changes of longitude and latitude into changes of right ascension and declination. Arguments, ☽'s longitude and latitude.

FORMULA: $d\alpha = \delta v + (v.a)\delta v + (\beta.a)\delta\beta$;
$d\delta = \delta\beta + (v.\delta)\delta v + (\delta.\delta)\delta\beta$.

☽'s long.	(v.a) β = −5°	0°	+5°	(β.a) β = −5°	0°	+5°	(v.δ)	(δ.δ)	☽'s long.
270	+ .133 +	+ .000 +	+ .050 +	.000	.000	.000	.000	.000	270
275	.131	.069	.049	− .043 +	− .041 +	− .040 +	+ .038 −	− .001 −	265
280	.126 +	.084 +	.045 +	− .085 +	− .081 +	− .079 +	.075 −	− .003 −	260
285	+ .117	+ .076	+ .039	− .126	− .121	− .117	+ .111 −	− .006 −	255
290	.105	.066	.030	− .165	− .158	− .154	.147 −	− .011 −	250
295	.091 +	.055 +	.021 +	− .202 +	− .193 +	− .188 +	.180 −	− .016 −	245
300	+ .074	+ .041	+ .009 +	− .235	− .226	− .220	+ .211 −	− .023 −	240
305	.057	.027	− .003 −	− .265	− .256	− .250	.242 −	− .030 −	235
310	.039 +	+ .011 +	− .016 −	− .292 +	− .282 +	− .277 +	.269 −	− .037 −	230
315	+ .021	− .004 −	− .028 −	− .316	− .306	− .301	+ .293 −	− .044 −	225
320	+ .003 +	− .018 −	− .040 −	− .336	− .326	− .322	.315 −	− .051 −	220
325	− .014 −	− .032 −	− .052 −	− .353 +	− .344 +	− .340 +	.335 −	− .058 −	215
330	− .030 −	− .045 −	− .061 −	− .368	− .359	− .356	+ .352 −	− .064 −	210
335	− .044 −	− .056 −	− .070 −	− .379	− .371	− .369	.366 −	− .069 −	205
340	− .056 −	− .065 −	.077	− .388 +	− .381 +	− .379 +	.378 −	− .074 −	200
345	− .066 −	− .073 −	− .082 −	− .395	− .388	− .388	+ .386 −	− .078 −	195
350	− .074 −	− .078 −	− .085 −	− .399	− .394	− .394	.393 −	− .080 −	190
355	− .080 −	− .081 −	.085 −	− .401 +	− .397 +	− .399 +	.397 −	− .082 −	185
0	− .084 −	− .083 −	− .084 −	− .401	− .398	− .401	+ .398 −	− .082 −	180
5	− .085 −	− .081 −	− .080 −	− .399	− .397	− .401	.397 −	− .082 −	175
10	− .085 −	− .078 −	− .074 −	− .394 +	− .394 +	− .399 +	.393 −	− .080 −	170
15	− .082 −	− .073 −	− .066 −	− .388	− .388	− .395	+ .386 −	− .078 −	165
20	− .077 −	− .065 −	− .054 −	− .379	− .381	− .388	.378 −	− .074 −	160
25	− .070 −	− .056 −	− .041 −	− .369 +	− .371 +	− .379 +	.366 −	− .069 −	155
30	− .061 −	− .045 −	− .030 −	− .356	− .359	− .368	+ .352 −	− .064 −	150
35	− .052 −	− .032 −	− .014 −	− .340	− .344	− .353	.335 −	− .058 −	145
40	− .040 −	− .018 −	+ .003 +	− .322 +	− .326 +	− .336 +	.315 −	− .051 −	140
45	− .028 −	− .004 −	+ .021 +	− .301	− .306	− .316	+ .293 −	− .044 −	135
50	− .016 −	+ .011 +	.039	− .277	− .282	− .292	.269 −	− .037 −	130
55	− .003 −	.027 +	.057 +	− .250 +	− .256 +	− .265 +	.242 −	− .030 −	125
60	+ .009 +	+ .041	+ .074	− .220	− .226	− .235	+ .212 −	− .023 −	120
65	.021	.055	.091	− .188	− .193	− .202	.180 −	− .016 −	115
70	.030 +	.066 +	.105 +	− .154 +	− .158 +	− .165 +	.147 −	− .011 −	110
75	+ .039	+ .076	+ .117	− .117	− .121	− .126	+ .111 −	− .006 −	105
80	.045	.084	.126	− .079	− .081	− .085	.073 −	− .003 −	100
85	.049 +	.089 +	.131 +	− .040 +	− .041 +	− .043 +	+ .038 −	− .001 −	95
90	+ .050 +	+ .090 +	+ .133 +	.000	.000	.000	.000	.000	90
	β = −5°	0°	+5°	β = −5°	0°	+5°			☽'s long.

○